becoming princess charming

CREATING THE MAGICAL MINDSET FOR YOUR

HAPPILY EVER AFTER

becoming princess charming

CREATING THE MAGICAL MINDSET FOR YOUR

HAPPILY EVER AFTER

by morgan mckean

BECOMING PRINCESS CHARMING
COPYRIGHT © 2013 MORGAN McKEAN

All rights reserved. Published in the United States by Gilliard Media Group Publishing. No part of this book sample may be used or reproduced in any manner whatsoever without written permission except in the case of brief quotations embodied in critical articles and reviews. For information; Gilliard Media Group Publishing, 1006 Riverside Drive, Ste. 734, Toluca Lake, CA. 91602

This book is written for information purposes only. The author is an Intuitive Empath, and not a licensed medical professional. Hence, the content in this book should not be considered a substitute for the advice of a licensed physician.

All efforts have been made to ensure the accuracy of the information contained in this book as of the date published. The author and publisher expressly disclaim all responsibility for any adverse effects arising from the use of application of the information contained herein.

FIRST EDITION DECEMBER 2018
Library of Congress Cataloguing-In-Publication Data is available on request.
ISBN 97809983783-2-9

Cover Photo : Amy Nikki Photography
Printed in San Bernardino, California

BeingMorgan.com
@morganbmckean | #becomingprincesscharming

MEDIA + SPEAKING: please contact hello@beingmorgan.com
PUBLISHING + SALES: please contact info@gilliardmedia.tv

DEDICATION

This book is dedicated to every woman who bought the lies the media sold her, and that well-meaning friends and family told her, which eventually became the records she played in her head again and again, when it came to believing she didn't deserve her very own happily ever after!

And for Ashley, Katherine and Nicole, whose belief, support, and ability to catch typos at a single glance turned my random musings about spirituality and happiness into a book that could help any woman discover that she already is becoming princess charming.

becoming princess charming

TABLE OF CONTENTS

Introduction

becoming princess charming instructions 6

vocabulary fit for a princess 8

fun 11

food 41

fitness 75

men 105

money 147

meaning 199

introduction

Once upon a time, there lived a beautiful woman who knew who she was and what she wanted, and how to create those things in her reality. Her life was filled with miracle upon miracle as she learned how to manifest her desired experiences and release the ideas and beliefs that were blocking her happiness. Like many of us, there was a time when she let beliefs in lack and limitation distort her ability to create her fairytale as she wanted it to be. However, by taking the very journey that you are embarking on now, she was able to release her false beliefs and outdated programming, while shifting her thought-stream towards ideas of love, success, and happiness, as a way to live like Princess Charming, creating her own happily ever after.

Many, many years ago, I heard Dr. Wayne Dyer, otherwise known as the "Father of Motivation," say "Loving people live in a loving world. Hostile people live in a hostile world. Same world." While I was aware that my thoughts influenced my reality, I hadn't really given much consideration as to how my attitude, positive or negative, effected how I experienced the world around me. Although, when you think about it, people who are low energy or "grouchy" can always find something to complain about, while those who are high energy or 'happy' seem to always see the good in things. Then, as a part of my own self-reflective nature, I thought about my perspective of the world, and quickly determined that while I was somewhere in between, I could really afford to be more loving.

Intrigued with this concept, I focused on it for a time, ultimately deciding to take it on as a personal scientific experiment. I started by dedicating certain days to being loving, patient, and kind, no matter what, just to see if and how it would affect my reality. Other days, I would be far less diligent, allowing, and even purposely entertaining fearful ideas that could potentially frighten me if they came into existence. As you can probably imagine, what I noticed was this: while they weren't perfect, the days I kept myself in a kind and loving place, all of my experiences went better, and when I indulged in a more negative mindset, I was usually faced with more challenges.

On the surface, this may seem like a trivial experiment with somewhat obvious results however, sometimes a simple shift in our perception can create the biggest difference in our experience. Just think, if taking on the practice of being kind and loving could increase the quality of your day, and you began to string those better-quality days together, wouldn't that put you on the path to your happily ever after? This is just one way that simple shifts in our perception can change our life miraculously.

my story

Because I know how intimate personal transformation can be, I want to share a bit of who I am with you, so that you can better relate to me. I was born an Intuitive Empath, and first dipped my toe in the human-potential movement at the ripe old age of six, studying metaphysics and the theories of the Science of Mind. A philosophy started by Dr. Ernest Holmes that addresses how mind plays into everything we experience. The philosophy contends that by consciously choosing the thoughts we think and focusing only on those things that we want to experience, we can effectively influence our physical reality to unfold the way we wish. Given this understanding for how to create my life at such a young age, you might think my life has been a cake-walk... NOT! While it's nice to understand things in theory as a child, until you go out in the world and put those theories into practice under the strain of real life, including stress, bills, anxiety, hormones, peer pressure and human needs, desires and insecurities, all you really have are some pleasant words that sound nice together, or read well on a page.

Venturing out into the world, young, naive, and full of passion and fabulous ideas for living, I discovered that my programming wasn't really working for me, as my ego used my spiritual understandings to push me to believe in ideas that were often too big and risky. Hence, I would do such things as jump into ventures, trying to give full belief in their possibility, only to determine mid-stream that it was a bad move for me. Over the course of a decade, multiple versions of these situations provided me with one long stream of emotional experiments in low self-esteem, fear of failure, feeling unworthy, anxiety, and an over inflated ego. Lucky for me, though I didn't think so at the time, these limiting ideas I held about myself were all reflected back to me through a rolodex of employers, and girlfriends and boyfriends who used, abused, and exploited my dreams of a fairy tale reality, often leaving me with nothing more than a spotted toad to kiss.

So, how did my cycle of amphibian canoodling stop and my life as Princess Charming begin? Well, in 2004 I got pregnant with the baby who would become the catalyst for my life to get infinitely better, and who empowered me to create my very own Happily Ever After. Let me preface this by saying, at the time of my pregnancy, I was not on the mommy track, nor was it actually becoming a mother that led to my happiness. However, the emotional and spiritual metamorphosis that consumed me as a result of being responsible for the life of this beautiful, worthy human-being who needed my unconditional love, changed me completely. There's nothing like someone outside of you that needs you to focus on their needs instead of your own pity-party to wake you up in life.

While pregnant with my son, one of my favorite spiritual teachers, Dr. Wayne Dyer, made his way back into my world, and this time with a PBS special on the "Power of Intention," which I highly recommend watching. Being that I was stuck on bed rest for what seemed like an eternity, I got to know that special very well. The funny thing about spiritual truths is that no matter where you are on the path, they will continue to resonate with you, again and again.

So, as I watched that special for the sixth or seventh time, it dawned on me that my theoretical ideas for spiritual living had finally sunk in, as I realized that I really knew that thoughts were things, and that it was my attention to them that brought them into reality.

So, what does all of this mean for you?

Well, after a lifetime of inner work, studying, and self-discovery, I now live with the power and confidence of being princess charming, the woman who knows how to create her happily ever after just as she wants it to be. Accordingly, I take it as my personal responsibility to use my intuition, real world experiences, and spiritual understandings to enlighten every woman ready to embrace the power of her own spirituality, as she learns that she can really create her fairy tale just as she wants it to be.

With love,

Morgan

becoming princess charming instructions

Each chapter in this book represents a spiritual strategy session centered on a specific area of your life, including fun, food, and fitness, and men, money and meaning. In each session is a venture into a journey of self-discovery, as well as learning what it will take for you to become princess charming, including exploring your past programming, how you are currently creating your reality, and why you believe the things that you want will make you happy.

While you may choose to use this book however you wish, my recommendation is to read it from beginning to end, introducing yourself to new ideas and concepts that can expand your awareness. Then, go back through each session, one by one, engaging in the exercises to invite that deep transformation to change your life for the better - permanently.

Lastly, at the end of each session, you will see where I invite you to write your fairy tale as you want it to be in that area. I do this because putting your ideas on paper is the first step in manifesting your dreams into your physical reality.

what you'll need

While all the ideas we're exploring in our sessions together are simple, I would still suggest you bring the following to your princess work if you want to reach success:

- Desire to have a better life than the one you have today.
- Courage to let go of old programming that has you stuck.
- Commitment to your pursuit of happiness.
- Tenacity to reach your own truths.
- Ability to see life as an experiment in your own spiritual evolvement.

a few last-minute warnings

If you stay committed to the concepts and processes shared in this book, there are some things I need to warn you about:

- You will have less to worry about and will have to find other ways to occupy your time.
- You may wonder if your fairy tale will last and self-sabotage – My advice: DON'T!
- You will start living your passion, taking better care of yourself.
- You will meet (or keep) your prince charming and be well on your way to happily ever after.

a vocabulary fit for a princess

Any time we embark on a journey, including one of self-discovery, we need the necessary tools to reach our destination. Accordingly, I want to provide you with some princess charming vocabulary, as there are many words and ideas I will reference throughout our sessions together that may be new to you, and I want to make sure that you understand the terms, and how I'm using them.

collective consciousness :: The term collective consciousness was coined in psychology by the French sociologist, Emile Durkheim, to refer to the shared beliefs or moral attitudes which work as a unifying force within a society.

I use this term to refer to how and why you believe what you believe based on your societal programming.

miracle :: While most people have been taught to believe that a miracle is an extraordinary occurrence, produced by supernatural causes, in the life of princess charming, a miracle is an ordinary occurrence that happens when you apply extra thought and feeling towards creating a desired experience in your reality.

manifesting :: Manifesting is a term that has been most recently associated with the hype surrounding the Law of Attraction. However, put more plainly, when you manifest something, you are making evident your deepest intentions and beliefs through physical experiences in your reality.

programming :: Although you probably think of programming as something we do to our computers and other technology, each of us, from the time we're born, receives information about the ideas we should believe in from our caregivers, teachers, friends, and media, as to who we should be and what we should want if we want to get along in this society. This programming then influences our ideas, beliefs, and thought stream, which effects the way we create and experience our reality.

source energy :: I use the term source energy to refer to that which produced the original thought from which all other thoughts in our universe emanate. I believe source energy is the life force that sustains life in you, me, and the world, and connects us all. I also believe that whether you call it God, Allah, Divine Intelligence, Source Energy, or Ralph, it will respond to you in the same loving way, for love is its nature and the law by which it operates.

it's not who you are that holds you back,

it's who you think you're not!

~ author unknown

SESSION ONE

fun

imagination

you can make believe anything

including becoming princess charming

in order to make your dream come true

play it in your imagination until you know what to do

then collect all the evidence that supports your new story

and act like a princess charming accordingly

f u n

"Mirror, mirror on the wall... how can I be the happiest me after all?"

Well, I'm so glad you asked my dear, as we are going to cover that, and so much more. However, before we start trying on ball gowns or sliding on any jeweled slippers, I want to take a moment to welcome you to Becoming Princess Charming, and your journey to being the type of woman who creates her happily ever after. I'm so excited that you decided to show up for a front row seat, as we will be revealing a clearer picture of who you are being and how that affects your ability to be happy. When we get clarity as to who we are and what we want, we automatically produce more fulfilling life experiences. As we learn to create these happier experiences for ourselves, we develop the necessary skills to produce our fairy tale just like Princess Charming. Therefore, to begin your transformative makeover into being the kind of princess you want to be, we are going to take the first step by entering into the kingdom of your imagination.

your imagination serves as the mental blueprint for turning your dreams into reality.

Now, I know in this fast-paced, media-rich world, it would be easy to toss aside the idea of fairy tales and princess charming as frivolous notions from childhood, however, if you want to live the life of your dreams, the best way is to stimulate your imagination with fun and playful ideas for living. Every idea you have about your life is first rehearsed for plausibility in your imagination, as it is here that you play out scenes to contemplate your thoughts and ideas through mental imagery.

To better demonstrate how your imagination has a direct impact on your life experiences, I invite you to recall a recent event where everything had to go a certain way in order for you to be pleased with it. As your memory plays back the scene, notice how many of the things that showed up in your physical experience, were the exact ideas you gave the most attention.

This occurs because our imagination is like an internal storybook and stage — constantly allowing us to write, rehearse, and revise our ideas for living, with each idea coming to fruition to the degree that we believe in it. It is for this reason that I often refer to our imagination as an incubator for our dreams.

When we place an idea in our imagination and allow it to go through a repeated process of mental imagery, we develop the insights and beliefs necessary to manifest our desired experiences. Therefore, having the ability to use your imagination in a fun and positive way is essential to the magical creation of your fairy tale, and happily ever after.

glass slipper insight :: In order to help you capitalize on the power of your imagination, I've designed the following exercise for you to try:

Close your eyes and picture an incubator. It doesn't matter the color, shape, or size, just that it fully closes and has a warm cozy feeling inside. Once you have a clear image of this incubator, imagine a few idea seeds gestating comfortably in the center.

Now, as you look at these seeds, I want you to stretch your imagination to explore what types of experiences will come about from the fruition of each. If you're stuck for ideas, try choosing one for work, then health, then relationships, then money, and then romance.

Next, expand your mental imagery on any one idea or seed as far out as you can believe. When you do this, take note of how your imagination plays the same scenes back to you over and over again, until you are able to take an idea from the beginning to the end.

bonus work :: Once you've gone through the exercise, write down any inspiring thoughts or ideas you had that you may want to implement towards creating a better life for yourself.

While I know that one exercise isn't going to change your entire life, I offered it to you in order to help increase your awareness as to the power of your imagination, and how it impacts what you experience. Everything that has ever been created was done so by someone who entertained an idea with their mental imagery until they had enough belief and understanding to bring it into physical reality. Therefore, regardless of your current circumstances, when you focus on ideas that are more in keeping with how you want life to be, it inspires you to take action towards creating that reality. Additionally, when you better understand the incubation process involved with evolving your ideas into your physical experience, it usually decreases much of the fearful or negative thought streams that can show up when you begin creating your life as you want it to be.

what kind of spell are you under

As I'm sure by now you can see, your thoughts and imagination have a direct effect on your reality, but - do you know how your ideas for living came to be yours in the first place? Do you think that you were born believing in certain spiritual or social ideals, such as, if you want a happily ever after, then marriage and babies must be part of your fairy tale? Probably not. Much of what you have believed about yourself and what you want, has come from the external programming you've received. Now, before you put up your defenses about being programmed, let me remind you that just as we program our computers or other technology to perform to our specifications, so too, do we require programming in order to know what's expected of us to survive as human-beings. Therefore, no stigma or fear needs to be associated with the fact that you are programmed to understand the basics for living in a cooperative society. The importance however, of understanding that you are programmed, is that if you are entertaining old ideas that no longer support you in achieving your desired results, you are now in a position to replace them with better ideas that do.

In my experience, when most people first really understand that they believe much of what they do because of the programming they've received, after a moment or two of realization, they start to get excited to shift their thoughts to be more in line with their dreams. However, before we can get into shifting your thinking, you're going to need to understand more about the programming process. When we're born, outside of our DNA and innate personality, we are pretty much a blank canvas in terms of what we believe about ourselves and our being here. It is on this blank slate that our first caregivers begin doing our programming, as they shared their culture, language, diet, and certain spiritual ideals, so that we would understand them and get along amicably in the family we were living with.

From here, our mental programming expands to include the concepts and ideas of educators and teachers, religious leaders, peers, and the media, each pushing their ideas or brand of programming for living on to us. Therefore, depending on the degree to which you question these types of things or have gone out into the world to explore your own ideas, much of what you believe it takes to live happily comes from the repetitive programming you received from your childhood, usually leading up into your twenties and thirties.

the programming we receive affects what ideas we choose to believe

Everything you want, you want because you believe it will make you feel happy, however, many of those ideas for happiness were given to you by someone else. As you can see, by exploring the concept of personal programming, often times the job, relationship, home, or social circle you desire is such because of the ideas fed to you thus far in your life. Because you have believed these particular ideas for happiness and successful living for so long, it may not have occurred to you how many of your pursuits might not be the things that will ultimately bring happiness to you. In order to help you see more objectively how various programming affects the ideas you play with in your mental imagery, I want to introduce you to three Princess Charmings. As each princess shares her story with you about how she lives now and the ideas that went into her initial programming, I want to remind you that there is no "correct" way to live; as living the life of Princess Charming means choosing those ideas that will bring you the most purpose, peace, and happiness.

conservative carmen ::

So far, my life has been pretty predictable. After graduating in the top five percent of my class from an Ivy League University, I took an internship as a junior accountant at one of the most prestigious firms in the area. While there,

I met my now husband, as he was working as an attorney in the same office building. After dating a few years, we got married, and shortly thereafter, our daughter was born.

I stayed at home with her for a while, but, now that she's in school all day, I've recently gone back to work full-time. Things have been a bit chaotic during our transition, but, to tell you the truth, it's been nice to get back to "being me," and with my full time salary, we'll be moving into that desirable new neighborhood soon.

her princess programming :: Outside of the fact that my parents got a divorce when I was still in elementary school, my childhood was pretty solid and stable. My mom remarried a decent guy who constantly reminded us about the importance of an education and our connection as family. My dad was much stricter than my mom, and outside of his live-in girlfriend, did everything by the book. From a young age, it was pressed upon me to "always do the right thing," and to invest my money wisely, or things wouldn't go well for me. Though they may be a bit straight and narrow, these ideas for living have guided me on almost every major decision, because I know that if I follow the "right path," everything will turn out okay.

how she imagines her happily ever after :: I guess I dream about the same thing that most women do. I imagine my daughter graduating from a good school. I love my work, as I'm right where I thought I would be on the corporate ladder, poised to make partner in the next year or two. Everyone is in good health right now — knock on wood, and I pray every day to keep it that way. Lastly, while my husband and I are pretty good friends, most of the time, I often wish there was more love or passion between us — so I often indulge in "steamy" romance novels and chick flicks. That said, I hope to make it till death do us part, as going through the stickiness of a divorce is so embarrassing for everybody.

liberal libby ::

I have lived more life in the last fifteen years than most people do in a lifetime. I've had several jobs, traveled back and forth across the country, not to mention internationally, and have had enough lovers to make the average woman blush. I'm grateful for all my experiences, but, I have to say the one I'm most proud of is my son. I met his dad on one of my many wild adventures, and after our affair ended, we never kept in touch, however, he gave me the amazing gift of motherhood. Because of my little bambino, I've settled down long enough to discover that you can have roots and wings, if you create your life out of love. Today, I have a great job teaching art, while selling my own work to local art galleries. My son goes to one of those "mind-body-spirit" schools and is practicing to be a marine biologist.

And my live-in boyfriend is definitely my best friend, and the nicest "step-dad" I could ever ask for.

her princess programming :: To say that I had an unconventional childhood would be defining my up-bringing mildly. Sure, my parents are still together to this day, but that's just because they spent the first part of their relationship making love not war while high on various substances, and the second part trying to recapture those "blissed out" moments. Our house was the local commune, as we had people of all ages, races, and multiple spiritual ideas staying with us. One week we would be entertained with the Hindu chants of Bhajan while eating vegan Indian food and the following week would be filled with vastly opposing ideas from Christians and psychics — now that was an interesting mix. No matter who I wanted to be or what I wanted to do with my life, I was always taught to follow my bliss - and that happiness is the way - so don't go chasing things outside yourself to make you feel happy.

how she imagines her happily ever after :: My dream is to have a big home over-looking the ocean where all of my friends and family can happily spend time together. In the backyard, I would have an indoor, outdoor art studio, as well as an organic garden to feed all those I love. My art would be featured in some of the world's finest galleries, and sometimes, I believe I'll even write a book about my traveling adventures. Of course, I want my son to have access to every idea that would bring him health and happiness. As for a romantic relationship, sometimes I enjoy them, but sometimes I enjoy my freedom more. Accordingly, the best guy for me is the one who loves me and gives me the freedom to show up in our relationship as who I want to be.

moderate molly ::

Sometimes, I believe I'm one of the luckiest girls in the world, as I am a partner in a successful public relations firm that specializes in the women's self-empowerment market. The way I got here is a bit of a fluke, as my career started off with me traveling the globe talking to women empowerment groups. During one of my trips through South America, I happened to be speaking about what it means to be a feminist in a male dominated society, and in the audience was my now business partner, taking in every word I was saying.

Long story short, she was a highly coveted P.R. guru, and today we run one of the most in demand firms in our niche. Of course, my parents are both proud of me – my father for becoming financially successful and my mother for picking up where she left off in her quest for women's equality. And yes, for those of you wondering, there is a man in my life, and while I love him, and he treats me impeccably, there's a lot more I want to do before I settle down with anyone steady.

her princess programming :: My childhood was mostly stable, but, sometimes a bit crazy. Before she met my father, my mother was a bit of a bra-burning, feminist hell-raiser. Whether it was fighting for women to get contraceptives or supporting local female politicians, my mother's passion to make sure women were seen as equals was unparalleled. Enter in my dad, who, while he agreed that women deserved better treatment, was more interested in keeping up appearances for people who would potentially be clients at his mortgage broker business. Together, they made quite a pair - she would tell me never bow to any man, and he would tell me that the kind of woman my mother wanted me to be is the kind that men avoid because they figure they can't make them happy. The one thing they could both agree on however, was for me to make sure I could take care of myself, so that I could choose a man because I wanted him, and not because I needed him to take care of me.

how she imagines her happily ever after :: Well, of course my top priority is expanding my business as far as I am able, which may or may not include merging with an even bigger agency. Either way, I want to be known as the go-to-person for some of the world's largest companies associating with the female self-empowerment market. I know I'll settle down, eventually, as I can tell at some point I'm going to want to have a family. However, before I can wrap my head around thinking about any of those things, I want to do something that I feel really defines me - whether it's an award-winning communications campaign or maybe becoming the chairperson of a large non-profit organization that supports women's causes, I need to create something that I and others can believe in.

glass slipper insight :: When reading about each of these Princess Charmings, were you able to see how their childhood programming had a direct effect on what they believed would bring them success and happiness?

Did you also notice how much of that same programming was further impacting their thought stream, even while they were imagining ideas for their future happily ever after?

Now that you are able to more clearly see how your programming effects your ideas for living, can you think of some ideas you believed about being happy up until now, that might be time to release?

While your programming may not be identical to any of the Princess Charmings here, I'm sure upon reflecting on their stories you were able to see where you also draw upon the programming you've received in order to create your life experiences. The reason being is this - you can only produce ideas for how you want your life to be by drawing from the ideas and things you've already been exposed to in consciousness. If you haven't been exposed to a particular thing or way of being, there is little if any reason to believe you would desire it.

life is the mirror that reflects our imagination back to us

Imagine for a moment that you are looking into a mirror that reflects your ideas instead of your physical being - the positive and negative, the beautiful and horrific - as the only things that this mirror can reflect are the ideas you believe in.

As you further gaze into your reflection and see the many ideas that your imagination is entertaining, you will notice how each expands and contracts according to the amount of attention and direction you give it. Now, to make this even more interesting, allow yourself to focus on one idea and watch how it unfolds scene-by-scene, just like watching a fabulous movie. As each scene plays out just as you expected, your experience of the imagery in this reflection is your mind's way of reaffirming back to you the validity of your beliefs and programming.

Being that it is so easy for us to get sucked into all sorts of programming, wouldn't it be amazing to have a mirror like this that was able to reflect back to you your ideas and beliefs so that you knew which ones would bring you the most fun, success, and happiness? Here's the good news . . . you do . . . it's called, your life! Your life, the one that you are physically experiencing, is nothing more than a reflection of the ideas that you entertain in your mind for living. For example, if you are the type of person who doesn't believe it's okay to eat fast food, chances are you wouldn't go into that type of restaurant. Equally true, if food isn't something that matters that much to you, you probably don't see much harm in ordering from the drive thru menu. Hence, if you are trying to better identify what you really believe, star t by taking inventory of the things that you're creating in your physical reality.

casting a new spell

If you've never been exposed to these types of ideas before, this could all feel a bit overwhelming. However, let me reassure you - once you understand that your beliefs are merely a result of past programming you've received, shifting your thought stream towards new ideas can be fun, to say the least. The gift in understanding your personal programming is being able to revise your ideas to better reflect the ways in which you want to experience your happily ever after. Because your imagination can only work with the types of ideas you feed it, if you currently believe in limitation, lack, victimhood, or fear, these are the types of ideas you will experience in your physical reality. This occurs so that you can understand your beliefs and who you're being more deeply.

In order to live the life of Princess Charming, you must first have some idea of how you want your fairytale to be, so that you can shift your thought stream accordingly — this is where the fun comes in. Now that you understand more about personal programming, you can more consciously choose all of the ideas that you feed into your imagination. The key to your success is honing your ability to tune into your current thought stream and identify those ideas that you want to expand in your reality.

The other important thing you want to be aware of is aligning yourself with those ideas, people, and organizations that resonate with the person you want to become so that you are constantly feeding your thought stream with new and improved ideas from which to create your reality.

On your journey to becoming Princess Charming we will explore many of your ideas, beliefs and programming, specifically as it relates to the areas of food, fitness, men, money, and meaning, so that we can see where your ideas are in line with your dreams, and where you may need to shift them a bit in order to experience your desired reality. To help jump start your magical mindset, I want to share with you some common ideas surrounding these areas, so that you can embark on a journey to see how simple it can be to begin shifting the ideas in your imagination in order to create your very own fairytale.

food :: Many of us are highly charged around the topic of food, as we need it for our survival and yet, too much or the wrong kind of it, or even too little or not enough of the right stuff, and we can become unhealthy - or at the least, our appearance can be altered in a way we don't quite want. Therefore, there is a usually a constant tug of war going on in our thought stream about what, and how much we can eat.

However, this tug of war only exists because of what we've been taught to believe about having a healthy relationship with food. In some cultures, it is considered sexy to be 30 to 40 pounds heavier than normal, as voluptuous women are highly coveted. In other cultures, it's more desirable to be physically fit - with definition in your arms, legs, and stomach, or some in which, yes, you can never be too thin. Accordingly, your judgment of your appearance, and how it effects what foods you eat is based heavily on the programming ideals of the culture you're in. However, what if you shifted your beliefs about food from worrying about your physical appearance to how it can keep your body healthy?

shifting your programming :: up until now, your beliefs about food have served you by bringing you to your current place of understanding, and if it's working for you, then great. If it isn't, and you're struggling in your relationship with food, then I invite you to try on the following shift in your programming. Food is not your enemy, nor is it something that you should be over indulging in or avoiding. Instead, try to think of your relationship with food as friendly - as it is this amazing sustenance that is only meant to sustain your body, keeping you alive and healthy. If you want to enjoy life to the fullest, you need to be as healthy as can be, and eating whole, organic foods that give your body what it needs, is the best way to keep yourself feeling happy.

fitness :: As part of keeping yourself healthy enough to take the journey of life, your body needs to be used physically, as neglecting it will cause it to atrophy. While working out wasn't as much a part of people's programming in generations past, because their daily routines were filled with more physical activity, our programming has made many of us much more sedentary. Now, it would be easy to blame our busy lives or not having enough money for a gym membership as our reasons for not being fit, however, the reason many of us play these ideas over and again, is because they let us off the hook for any heavy lifting (pun intended). What I believe is a bigger part of the missing piece isn't the excuses that we use to avoid our fitness routine, but, rather that we really don't believe, until a disease shows up, that our working out keeps us healthy.

shift in programming :: While some people are natural born athletes, loving every moment of using their body physically, many of us don't necessarily share that same enthusiasm. Therefore, we have to create some ideas and mental imagery that supports our new belief about taking physical fitness more seriously. When you realize that the quality of your life will greatly depreciate without a healthy body, dedicating yourself to working out a few times a week doesn't seem like such a big chore. One idea I've used to help people through their anxiety about committing to a sustainable fitness routine is by helping them choose something more in keeping up with their personality. If you're not a gym rat, don't join one. Instead, try hiking, walking, or biking, and if those don't float your boat, maybe swimming, rollerblading, dancing, or yoga would do the trick to increase your endorphins and keep you fit.

men :: Because all of us go into relationships with our various social programming, there is no doubt that we're going to have different ideas about how to maintain a successful relationship. Therefore, if you've never taken the time to explore the idea of personal programming, it would be very easy to make your man, or men in general, "jerks" for not living up to your expectations. However, when you step back from your emotional attachment to the outcome of an experience, you will realize that you are in a relationship with someone who has been programmed with all his own ideas for happiness. Accordingly, when you release the need for a man to read your mind or to deliver your happiness, you allow yourself to experience more peace, because now you don't have to get angry every time he doesn't show up according to your preconceived ideas.

shift in programming :: No matter how in sync you are with another person, because each of you is an individual, your ideas for living will always be unique. Living with one another more successfully, entails that you take into account that his internal programming for happiness is just as ingrained in his belief system as yours. Doing so will give you a better perspective from which to entertain mental imagery that includes space to consider your partner's' ideas and beliefs. By opening up the channel for the healthy discussion of ideas, beliefs, and programming, you release your partner from the "make- believe" ideals that you've been holding on to, while allowing space for him to contribute to your happily ever after with you.

money :: Like food, money is another highly charged issue in most people's lives, as our very ability to obtain the goods and services we need to survive depends on our ability to make it. However, it wasn't always this way, as over multiple generations, we have used a many means of exchange in order to get the things we want and need. So, why then, do so many of us believe that money is such a coveted thing? Like everything else we've discussed thus far, it all has to do with our programming. If you were like most children, your first introductions to money had to do with teaching you how valuable it is, as well as how hard it is to attain. If you're like most people, I'm sure you heard things like "Money doesn't grow on trees," which over time convinced you that money wasn't something that you were going to come by very easily. Therefore, if you want money to be part of your happily ever after, you're going to have to shift your imagination accordingly.

shift in programming :: While you may currently believe that money is something rather difficult to come by, repeatedly entertaining those ideas in your mind isn't going to create the happily ever after that you desire. Money - the paper, coins, and plastic we use as a means of exchange, all on its own, has little, if any value to us. Hence, the real charge we feel when we think of money is our connection to the things we want to attain with it. So, if what you want is to experience more money so that you can buy the things that bring you happiness, then these are the types of ideas that you must feed for your imagination to play with.

Start feeding yourself with ideas for all the ways that there is to make money and keep following each scene until you get the answer or lead that inspires you enough to believe. From here, take this idea and keep it in the forefront of your thinking, until you are taking the "right" action to experience making more money in your reality.

As I mentioned earlier, these ideas are fairly generalized, as I realize that the experiences you are currently facing are potentially much more complex. However, my reason for introducing them to you is to start your mind thinking about how many more ways there are to believe about you and your life. Just by daring to explore new ideas for living, you open yourself to experience a whole new world of possibilities. When you understand personal programming and how your imagination plays with your ideas to create your reality, you will then have the power to turn your best ideas for living into your life as Princess Charming.

if you're going to the ball, you're gonna have to get a dress

There's another aspect to the process of turning your ideas into reality that usually includes a little bit more effort than letting our imaginations entertain our ideas. No, I'm not pulling a bait and switch on you regarding the importance that your imagination plays in delivering your happiness, as it is the spark that lights the ignition.

However, once you are able to comfortably put together the scenes for your next desired experience, I'm going to invite you to do what I call "Acting as if." Just for the record, "Acting as if" is not the same as "Fake it till you make it," because if you tell your mind you need to "fake it to make it," you're also telling yourself that who you are now isn't good enough to experience your desired reality. That isn't the best way to increase your ability to believe in your dreams. If you're having a bit of a challenge understanding the difference, I'd like to further clarify by presenting it like this: If you knew - or had every reason to believe that you were going to a big event soon, in your anticipation you would begin your preparations, including getting a new dress. Therefore, as your actions would suggest, in both your imagination and in your physical activity, you are "acting as if."

Do you remember when I mentioned that entertaining playful and fun ideas about life was key to living the life of Princess Charming? Well, here is where we put the play into practice. As a child, you may remember pretending to be a teacher, a. doctor, or an airline pilot, just for the fun of it. However, playing pretend at that time was really serious business. In order to fulfill your desire to have the experience of being a particular person, you would put on any outfit, grab any prop, and persuade any person necessary to bring your idea to life. Now, as a grown up, you can still reach into your creativity by beginning to act like the person you want to be.

"Okay, While I'm starting to get this whole concept of acting as if, Morgan, can you please explain to me how pretending to be Princess Charming is going to make me feel happy?"

Becoming Princess Charming and creating your happily ever after as you want it to be is like taking the lead in your own movie, or taking full responsibility for your life. It is deciding who you want to be in order to experience happiness, and then reinforcing that idea in every way you can imagine, until it becomes a natural part of your being. Whether it's buying a new dress, writing out a business plan, or going to get your passport, the key to further reinforcing your new programming that you can be who you want to be, is by focusing in on those situations that would allow you to further express yourself as the you that you are becoming. This is because the main reason you want to be who you want to be, or want the things you want, is because you believe your experience of them will make you feel happy. Therefore, one of the best ways to accelerate the manifestation of a certain experience is to act as if your desires are coming into fruition.

This behavior solidifies your intention to bring the manifestation to life, hence fueling your imagination with the ideas it needs to create your perfect reality.

healthy ideas for 'acting as if'

When you begin acting like the person you want to become, here are some questions to ponder on while shifting your thought stream.

If I'm being who I want to be....

How would I treat myself and others?
How would I spend my work days and free time?
Who would my friends be?
Would I have more confidence?
Would I be nicer to people?
Would I spend more time with those I love?
Would I be healthy and happy?

Now, for every single answer you gave, I'm sure there is one thought, one idea, or one action step you can take towards creating deeper roots for that idea to show up in your reality.

One last reminder about successfully" acting as if". Before taking any serious action towards your desired reality, you want as much clarity as possible as to who you want to be. This ability to feel yourself as the person you want to be will elevate your mood and confidence, which will put you in closer resonance to bringing about your desire. It is from this expanded state of awareness as to who you will be, or how you will feel, when you experience your desired reality that inspires you to take the right steps towards bringing about your happiness.

avoid negative spell casting

Now that you understand how your programming and imagination work together to bring about the ideas that you focus on most intently, you must be careful not to throw anything in the mix that you don't really want to experience. The reason being is this - your imagination doesn't decipher whether or not an experience will be good for you before it begins entertaining it. Your imagination's only purpose is to help facilitate your ability to turn an idea into your desired experience, which it defines as any idea you give your attention to. Accordingly, if you place ideas in your mental imagery about fear and anger, you will create experiences in your physical reality that reflect this thinking. Hence, even when you're not focusing specifically on your dreams, you have to make sure that you're not entertaining ideas that will deter you from the type of life you want to experience. While it would be easy to believe you will never have a negative thought again, it's probably unrealistic. The fact is that many of us were taught to test our ideas by playing the worst-case scenario over again to see if we could handle it. Based on how much we've practiced this mental exercise, we've become experts at filling our imagination with stress and worry whenever we contemplate any new ideas for living. As you now know, this type of programming definitely affects your ability to create your reality as you want it to be, as your constant attention to negative details can only expand their existence in your experience. So, when choosing ideas to entertain about your fabulous new lover, ideal career, or perfect house, make sure that you get absolute clarity on what you want to experience, so you don't allow room for negative ideas to become present.

glass slipper insight :: A great way to alleviate your tendency to give energy to your negative or fear based ideas, is to eliminate all of your complaining, as well as any conversations with yourself, and others, that includes ideas such as:

- I don't deserve this.
- I'm not good enough for that!
- I'll never make enough to get the house/car/life of my dreams.
- Things always seem to be difficult for me.

"But Morgan, what if I've always spoken this way? What if I don't know how to stop thinking negatively, or at least a bit sarcastically?"

appreciation is the magic wand you've had all along

I understand how challenging it can be to step up to the idea of becoming Princess Charming, especially if you're used to thinking of yourself, or parts of your life, in a less than positive way. Therefore, before we close our first session together, I'm going to give you your own magic wand, the kind that can reverse your fears and stop the all the negative chatter. I'd like to call this magic wand, "appreciation." When you have appreciation, you're in one of the highest emotional states possible, which then increases the quality of your ideas for living considerably. When you are in a state of appreciation, you are focused on all of the many wonderful ideas that make up your reality. By deliberately blending appreciation into all of your ideas for the future, you will help your imagination bring forth the type of stories that are most suitable for your happily ever after.

No matter what kind of fairytale you're currently in, being in appreciation for you and for your life will deepen your feelings of peace and increase your clarity. This clarity and peace allow you to see all the beauty and truth in your world, which in turn allows you to think of better ideas in order to make up your future reality.

When you are in a state of victimhood or fear, all your ideas for living will create experiences that reflect this to you. However, when you are in a state of appreciation, rather than being reactive when things don't go exactly as you plan from moment to moment, you are able to stay clear, as you go with the flow, trusting that eventually, your happiness will be delivered to you, just like in a fairy tale. If you really want to be Princess Charming, one of the most powerful things you can do is appreciate all the good you see in your current reality, as this will help you succeed on your journey to creating your happily ever after.

glass slipper insight :: One of the best ways I know to turn your fairy tale into reality is to write it, as your story becomes the map which guides you to your happily ever after. Accordingly, I invite you to now begin writing out your ideas for how you want your life to be as you Become Princess Charming.

Write your new story or some ideas that you want to bring into your reality the kind you can believe in:

_____
_____
_____
_____

one last thought before we move on to the fountain of food

Once upon a time, a beautiful woman believed that she could become Princess Charming - so, she placed every pleasant idea she could think of in her imagination in order to create her happily ever after, just as she wanted it to be. ~ M

SESSION TWO

food

you nourish me

you comfort me

and you provide me energy

you distract me

you satisfy me

and you keep me company

food

"You are what you eat!"

When you read that phrase, does it bring you feelings of comfort or fear?

Great! Now we've got a place from which to start your new relationship with food.

I was going to begin our session together by reminding you that we're all living life at a much more hectic pace, trying so hard to keep up with our job, friends, family, events, and social media that trying to fit in a healthy meal, barely makes our radar. But, I'm going to assume you already know all that, and get into what I believe our experience of food is and how we relate to it in our daily lives.

From the time we're babies, up until the time we become small children, most of us have a very healthy relationship with food, choosing to eat only when we're hungry and quitting when we get full. But, through a process of experience and reflection our programming or beliefs about what food is evolves, and our relationship with food changes. While there is no specific age at which this programming starts, it seems to begin with how our parents and first caregivers personally valued food, and then used it as a means to get us to behave the way they wanted us to.

Because much of our programming about food in Western civilization seems to be shared as a collective consciousness, I'm going to use some of the more stereotypical ideas or phrases we hear, and their general feeling or meaning, in order to help bring your awareness to where some of your first programming about food may have originated from.

phrase :: Finish your plate, there are people starving in the world!

general feeling or meaning :: I believe in lack and limitation - if you don't eat that food, you're wasting the limited amount of energy I have to buy, prepare, and serve it to you. Have some gratitude and appreciation for how hard I'm working to provide for you.

reality :: Yes, there are people starving in the world, and the belief or energy supporting that idea can't fade away quick enough however, eating the last bite of food on our plate is not going to help that child starving half way around the world.

phrase :: If you're a good girl, you'll get a cookie, happy meal, or treat!

general feeling or meaning :: I really need you to conform fully to my vision for your behavior in this situation. I am willing to "reward you" with something I know gives you immediate satisfaction, in order to get you to do what I want you to.

reality :: Using rewards to teach children good behavior is part of "Human-Being Training 101." Using sugary processed foods as a reward however, might not always be the wisest long-term choice, as we tend to reward ourselves in the same way our parents did over and again for much of our lives. Therefore, Reward = Junk Food, may not be the most positive programming to reinforce.

phrase :: Do you know how long I slaved over a hot stove to make you that food? You better finish that whole plate!

general feeling or meaning :: I am identifying how you feel about me personally with whether or not you want to eat the food I prepared. Right now, I see your purpose as someone to validate me and my existence by eating that food.

reality :: There are times that each of us will identify with something we've created, or take personally when someone rejects our ideas. However, inflicting our current fragile mood onto others is not going to bring us the real self-respect and self-validation that will allow us to once again feel whole.

glass slipper insight :: If reading any of those statements caused emotionally charged energy to come up, take a moment to feel whatever it is, maybe jot it down, and then when you're ready, keep going.

I'm sure, in reading each of those ideas you felt a certain set of emotions, ranging anywhere from anger, frustration, sadness, relief, and indifference. However, no matter where you find yourself on the emotional scale, the one place I don't want you to sign on to is the "blame-train." In order to avoid this space, I invite you to take a moment to fully realize that no one outside of you created those experiences with the intention of causing you any harm - they were simply reacting to their own perspective about how to best deal with a situation they were being presented. Their perspective, and the subsequent ideas for their course of action, were originally formulated by their parents and caregivers, who probably knew no better themselves. Hence, each caregiver did what they knew to be best at the time and hating or blaming them is like you drinking poison and expecting the other person to die. It just won't work!

Just so we're clear, the reason that I drew your attention to the above programming ideas wasn't for you to start wallowing in self-pity about anything that was taught to you. I said it for the sole purpose of creating the awareness that if your current relationship with food is a result of all of the programming you've received up until now, then you can start reprogramming it today as you want it to be.

With that in mind, let's take a moment to establish what your relationship with food is, so that the reprogramming can begin.

what's my current relationship with food

In this exercise, I want you to read and answer each of the following questions from your current level of understanding, with complete authenticity and total compassion for yourself. Then continue reading. When you have completed this chapter, I invite you to come back to these same questions and answer them again to see if your perspective on any of these ideas has shifted one way, or another.

- What do I enjoy most about the eating process?
- When I think of food, what types of ideas, thoughts, feelings, and beliefs arise?
- Do I use food for anything other than a source of fuel to keep me going?
- Am I aware of any external triggers that cause me to eat unnecessarily?
- What are my favorite foods (the ones I really eat the most), and why?
- How do I want to feel after I eat a typical meal?

what your plate says about you

Every plate of food you choose to eat tells a story about who you are "being" in that moment. If that sounds a like a lot, let me further explain. Every choice we make originates from who we are being, whether it's how we choose to wear our hair or which girlfriend we call to get advice from; our ideas and motivations for living come from our perspective and level of consciousness. Therefore, when we are experiencing a low mood, which usually means we're feeling spent or weak, we usually opt for sugary, salty, or highly processed foods to increase our serotonin and bring us comfort. The same is true for our other states of being. When we are experiencing a high mood from good feelings, it usually means we may be more mindful to keep our healthy state of being by choosing whole, unprocessed foods. if we're somewhere in between, our plate would reflect a combination of choices.

Take for instance a meal consisting of lemon water, with a whole food salad, a fatty, calorie rich dressing, and a side of French fries. The story we are creating behind a plate like this is that we're "being" someone who wants to move towards a better relationship with food and our body, but still has a little way to go.

In order to help you further understand how who you are being has a direct effect on how you relate to food, I want to introduce you to the following stereotypical eaters. Whether or not you've met them before isn't as important as what this amazing group of women, who are also "becoming princess charming" can potentially show you about yourself.

fast food frieda ::

Most of you have known me, at least at some point in your life. I'm always on the go because I've got a super hectic life. If I'm not picking up fast food at the drive- thru window on my way home from work, I'm definitely picking up a sugary coffee drink and a donut at the local coffee house the next morning.

I see food as a way to keep my stomach from growling, and whatever's most convenient is what I grab. A more aware version of me, who is a little more weight conscious, may use a lot of meal replacement bars, and diet, processed convenience foods.

what my current eating style says about who I am being :: I keep my life super busy so that I don't have to think about anything, including what I'm eating for lunch, at a deep level. By staying on a proverbial "treadmill," I don't have time to (want to) evaluate the parts of my life that aren't pleasant, as I pile more and more stuff on the ever expanding 'to-do' list that I'll never catch up on because then I would have to "feel stuff." Because my first goal is to feel happy, or to not feel much of anything at all — eating feel-good foods that are fast and convenient are a great fit with my go-go-go lifestyle!

starving sarah ::

It saddens me to think how many of you may know me far more intimately than I wish. To people who see me, I may look healthy or at least thin. However, I really see food as the enemy, something I will only eat to keep myself from starving, or maybe not even then. Like a lot of women, it started out when I wanted to drop a few pounds to look good for an upcoming event, and then somewhere along the way, I got this feeling of power that I could actually control my weight through starvation. Because everyone has been starting to question how much I'm eating lately, I've begun playing around with eating and then regurgitating my meals. It's not the sexiest way to maintain my weight but, at least I look good, for now anyways.

what my current eating style says about who I am being :: I live in a world of fear, self- loathing, and denial. I am a consummate perfectionist, always trying to live up to the version of me that the media and people tell me I need to be in order to be loved and accepted. I live my life on eggshells, highly insecure in my peer group and romantic relationships, afraid that if I don't look or act "right" my friends or partner will abandon me. Additionally, my endless need for outside approval and validation from others ends up suffocating anyone who shows me the least bit of attention. I may be miserable but, at least I look good, right?

ego eater edna ::

I'm sure, if you're like many of the women in the U.S., you know me all too well. I say I eat healthy all the time, and if I don't look too closely at what I actually put into my mouth, I would almost believe it to be true. Whether it's dining with the girls at the local organic restaurant or switching out my white rice for brown, on an intellectual level, I believe I'm doing what is necessary in order to be healthy. However, what I don't like to admit to is that when I buy a cart of healthy groceries, and I then add more than a few processed treats, along with a diet soda and candy bar, right before I leave the checkout counter. Also, I would never even think to admit to the fact that I grab a sugar latte drink almost 5 days a week, often pairing it with a processed sugary thing-a-ma-bob.

what my current eating style says about who I am being :: I am usually a little more appearance than substance oriented, ego driven, and very reliant on the opinions of others to validate my choices. I typically follow the (materially) successful crowd's opinion because I'm either part of that crowd myself or working hard to be. I know eating well and working out are healthy for my body, and while I do appreciate those benefits, my main reason for doing all this stuff is to look good.

perfectionist polly ::

I think only a few of you could possibly know me, after all, how many people can live up to perfection? I am totally perfect in my food choices. I'm on a whole food, plant based, organic raw food diet. I drink the recommended amount of water daily, and never drink alcohol or indulge in anything that would ever potentially have a negative impact on my body. I've also given up sugar, gluten, dairy, and any of the other things the holistic health world is currently saying isn't in line with total health. Sure, it takes a lot of discipline to live this way but, if you want total health, this is how to do it.

what my current eating style says about who I am being :: I typically have a rather black and white approach to life. Things either are or they're not, there's not much room for gray. While it may look to an outsider that this is all about being healthy, what I'm hoping they can't see is my fear about life. I live and eat this way because to do anything short of hitting the mark would cause me (un)known pain and suffering that I don't want to deal with. Therefore, to make authentic choices that honor how I'm feeling, rather than what the "rules" tell me to do, is not an option. Even if this all seems difficult to someone else, by living my life by a strict code, I experience the feeling of enough control to help me best manage my life. Plus, the pay of here is my body really is perfect!

work in progress peggy ::

More and more of you are getting to know me every day, which couldn't thrill me more. For the most part, I no longer make food choices, healthy or unhealthy, based on my ego. While not all areas of my diet are perfect, those parts that I need to address most are the ones that are receiving most of my attention. When I grocery shop for my family, I make as many organic choices as my market options and budget will allow. Every once in a while, I get sweets and treats but, I've still got myself on a steady path to good nutrition.

what my current eating style says about who I am being :: I am really beginning to listen to myself and my authentic being. I've developed the foundation for a healthy self-esteem, and while I am still attached to many conventional ideas about life, positive and negative, I'm starting to explore new concepts about myself, my values, and who I want to be moving forward. I'm not claiming to be perfect – far from it. However, I am realizing on a very deep level that if I want to experience transformation in my world, I must take responsibility for creating my desired experiences.

So, did you recognize yourself in any of those women? Maybe a little bit of each, to differing degrees?

Hopefully, in taking the time to get to know each of them a little more intimately, you were able to make a direct correlation on how who we are being has a direct effect on our perception of what food is, and our subsequent relationship to it. It is through this process that you will gain a better understanding of the motivations that drive you towards eating food, outside of an empty belly that is.

glass slipper insight :: To get clearer about your relationship with food, ask yourself the following... What is my current eating style, and what does it say about who I'm being?

When we keep our focus on being our best selves, we often feel clear, happy, and supported by life, which decreases our need for external stimuli in order to positively shift our mood. However, when we focus on lesser ideas about who we are, we usually "feel bad," and therefore, look to outside distractions in order to cope through our feelings. The better you are able to fully come to this realization, the more fluidly you will be able to consciously and deliberately create your own future story with food.

For the record, while I understand that some of you choose to demonstrate your being as the "queen of will power," I do not advocate this methodology for controlling your eating, and here's why. When you fight against the person that you are being in the moment, you will experience internal conflict. The whole reason we create an experience is to be able to reflect upon who we are being. It is from this perspective that we can decide whether or our thought stream is leading us to our desired result.

glass slipper insight :: When you reflect upon an experience, in order to decide if you are aligned with your best and highest "being," ask yourself, "Did I achieve my desire?" If yes, then continue along that same thought stream, refining as necessary. If no, then to the degree that it was off, you must go back to the drawing board (your imagination) in order to reformulate a new idea - one that better reflects your desired vision.

When you acknowledge who you are being first, you will be more equipped to make food choices that benefit your entire "being," rather than giving into immediate gratification in the moment. In other words, actively pursuing the path to your happily ever after will naturally assist you in making better choices when it comes to your relationship with food, as well as helping you to take your power back as the amazingly fabulous woman you are.

creating a better relationship with food

I believe that most of us try to operate with the best information available. However, in order to expand our consciousness to the next level of understanding, we usually need to connect with someone who knows more than us. When we were children, these people were easy to identify, as they were our parents, relatives, and other grown-ups, who we just knew had all the answers when it came to creating their very own happily ever after. However, now that we're the grown-ups, who is here to help parent us, and provide us with the tools we need to help reprogram our minds so that we can experience a life of our own design? *We are, that's who!*

That's right, it's time to play I can be my very own Fairy God Mother...

It's true, right now you have the magical power to begin to shift your relationship with food. To start, I would like to invite you to take a moment to remember how your mother provided you with your original programming (beliefs). Imagine for example, how she went about teaching you the importance of dental hygiene by reminding you to brush your teeth every day - morning and night, and possibly after every single meal. It probably seemed like if she told you once, she told you a million times but, there was some magic that occurred through the process of her repetition. If I asked you about how ingrained it is in your head to brush your teeth twice a day, and after meals when you can your answer would be, "of course."

EXACTLY! As I'm sure at this point, there is no question in your mind that taking care of your teeth is the royal way to maintain a healthy mouth.

When you received your initial programming about any task or behavior as a child, if you can recall, there were days that doing it seemed easy and light, and others, a dread. Therefore, it was only through your intention and the diligent repetition of the behavior, and not by giving in to your various mood swings, that you learned to make it part of your being. Accordingly, it is my recommendation that when it comes to reprogramming your beliefs, begin by being gentle with yourself, compassionately deciphering how your various emotions effect your ability to obtain your goals, rather than creating distractions to muffle their effects. When you do this, you will discover whatever it is that you believe is really lacking in the moment, along with the opportunity to address it, instead of turning to the distraction to cope. The payoff to fully grasping this understanding is this: when you learn that this type of repetition of a particular idea works to create one set of programming, you can duplicate and apply it to achieve your desired result in other areas of your life.

The path to your happily ever after is very much one of self-discovery - one that requires you to have the courage to ask yourself who you are being, what you want to experience, and how to use your beliefs and emotions as tools to help you get there. Our emotions are not meant to be suppressed but, rather to serve us like an internal GPS system, guiding us towards the things we want while deterring us away from the things we don't. When we pay attention to them in this way, instead of trying to suppress them with food or other outside stimuli, they lead us right to our desired experience or our Happily Ever After!

Are you beginning to see the simplicity of all of this? You have it within you to be your very own Fairy God Mother, writing your own fairy tale and granting your own wishes as you choose. You can access your innate wisdom to gently guide you to your most authentic being, and those results that will bring you the most happiness.

now is the time to let go of those ideas that no longer serve you.

"Well, that all sounds great in fairy la la-land Morgan, but,"

- I don't care about being a fairy godmother - I just don't want to feel yucky.
- I work too many hours to even think about eating right, let alone "parent myself."
- This is how I've always been, and I really don't believe I can change.
- I'm going through a bad break up - I'll start taking care of myself as soon as I recover from it.

I get it... I really do... and here's what I will say to that:

"If you always do, what you've always done, when it comes to taking care of your health, you're likely to get a little less return on your effort than the time before because your body is aging, and doin' the same old same old won't even keep you in as good of condition as you are now."

Now then, if you are ready for change... if you really want to create your happily ever after, then I invite you to deepen, soften, and open just a little bit more to allow a new version of you to emerge.

To make things simple, I've created some foundational ideas to inspire you to create new ways of thinking about your relationship with food, and the emotional triggers that typically set you off. My hope is that by creating the awareness in you to pause, so that you can figure out what the emotion you are feeling is REALLY trying to tell you, you will be able to access better coping skills than eating through the experience.

reprogramming your thoughts & feelings around food

understanding :: I am "feeling" LONELY because I feel emptiness or separation from others. I feel this separation because it is what I am choosing to demonstrate in this moment by way of my thoughts and beliefs about myself, and my world. By choosing to be someone who acknowledges that there is nothing to be separate from, I can begin to reestablish my feelings of connection to everyone and everything around me.

what to do :: **When I feel lonely,** instead of coping with the moment by eating food, I will find a way to experience more love by giving it away. I will do this through connective activities I enjoy such as volunteering my time to worthy causes, calling a friend to check on them, taking a group exercise or yoga class, playing or supporting my child, or helping someone in need.

understanding :: I am "feeling" HAPPY because I feel connected, loved, and in total alignment with who I say I am being in the moment. Because I want to continue these feelings of happiness, I may be tempted to overindulge in feel good foods. However, because I understand that my thoughts fuel my feelings of happiness, I am able to remind myself that I don't need food to maintain my connection.

what to do :: **When I feel happy,** instead of focusing on food as the only way to celebrate, or as the main feature of a celebration, I will incorporate fun activities such as dancing, engaging conversation, and connective games with others to maintain or enhance my mood.

understanding :: I am "feeling" BORED because I do not feel connected to source energy, and therefore don't feel inspired to express my creativity by either creating a way to bring an idea into physical form or coming up with an activity to entertain myself.

what to do :: **When I feel bored,** instead of using food as a means of distraction, I will summon up whatever creativity is available to me by demonstrating it in the most simple of ways, including reading a book, writing a gratitude list, going for a walk, creating an original piece of art, cleaning the house (hey, it keeps it clean and burns calories) or inspiring others with my amazingly clever social media postings.

understanding :: **I am "feeling" SAD/DEPRESSED** because I am experiencing a varied combination of feelings which probably includes fear, lack, loss, and disconnection from love. I don't know what to think or feel in order to restore peace to my being, which now leads me to use food as my pacifier. While food may feel like a source of comfort, I will now allow myself to take the necessary steps to bring true healing where I am currently feeling loss.

what to do :: **When I feel sad/depressed,** because I know I am in a fragile state of mind, the first way I will reaffirm love in my life is by being kind and gentle with myself. I will also place myself in supportive environments, which includes the company of loving family and friends, who care about my well-being, and who can hold space for me when I am feeling low. I will also stock my space with healthy food options, knowing that my energy is vibrating at a low frequency and that I need healthy nourishment as I process who I am currently being. While I may not be able to change everything all at once, I can begin to place small goals in front of me to once again restore my feelings of peace, love, and harmony.

I know the above examples may not cover every emotion that you will ever feel, however, my hope is that by sharing with you some of the more common triggers, and possible resolutions to those triggers, you can further shift your relationship with food into a healthy one. Additionally, in order to help further root these new ideas and coping tools into your thought stream, I invite you to come up with potential ideas, solutions, and tools that may serve you when you find yourself in one of these states of mind.

Next to the following emotions, come up with one or two ways you could express yourself in a healthy way that doesn't require food.

example :: When I am Being someone who feels Lonely, I will blast out a text message to my closest girlfriends to see who can go on a walk with me, and if no one is available, I'll go to a yoga class to shift my mood.

When I am being someone who feels Anxious, I_____

When I am being someone who feels Love, I _____

When I am being someone who feels Abandoned, I _____

When I am being someone who feels Happy, I _____

When I am being someone who feels Rejected, I _____

When I am being someone who feels Success, I _____

When I am being someone who feels Failure, I _____

When I am being someone who feels Bored, I _____

When I am being someone who feels Angry, I _____

simple steps for mindful eating

Take a moment of gratitude before eating.

Set specific, uninterrupted time for meals, even just 10 - 15 minutes.

No multi-tasking while eating - no emails, television, texting or smart phone.

Chew your food slower, and more completely,

Contemplate taste, texture, and thoughts that come up as you eat.

Wait several minutes to see if you're still hungry before taking a second helping.

so what does a princess eat

While I'm not claiming to be a nutrition expert, I have been learning about the power of food from holistic health practitioners since I was a young child. I have demonstrated vibrant health most of my life, and if you've met me, you know that I have more energy than a five-year old pumped up on caffeine and sugar, with no outside stimuli. Therefore, I feel I know more than a few basics when it comes to eating well and wanted to share with you what I do know about certain foods, and how they can positively or negatively affect your body. However, if you have specific health concerns or questions on what foods work best with your body type and lifestyle needs, I highly recommend searching out a certified health consultant or there are several Do-It-Yourself options you can research online.

"Let food be thy medicine and medicine be thy food."
~ Hippocrates

No matter what your food preferences, I always advocate for a whole food diet, as it offers our bodies the most efficient fuel to maintain our being at optimum health. If you are unfamiliar with what a whole food diet means, the term is meant to define those foods that are unprocessed, unrefined, or processed and refined as little as possible before consumption. Whole foods typically do not contain added ingredients such as salt, fat, sugar, artificial ingredients, or even supplemental vitamins. Examples of whole foods include fruits and vegetables, unprocessed meat, poultry and fish, unpolished grains and unprocessed dairy products.

As you can see, the basics of a whole food diet are pretty simple, right? Eat fruits, vegetables, nuts, freshly harvested beans (the dry kind - not canned), animal-protein and non-homogenized milk and dairy products.

"But, Morgan... what about my bread, pasta, rice and cereal, am I going to have to give all that up?"

The short answer is "No." However, I do recommend making some changes to the quantities and qualities of the bread and rice products you consume. For example, instead of eating white or sourdough bread, choose a multi-grain or whole wheat bread, and instead of eating white rice, switch over to brown, or a more protein rich grain like quinoa. It may take a little while to get use to all of these shifts in your diet, so to start, I want to encourage you to take small, reasonable steps, making just a few manageable changes at a time so that you are able to establish a solid foundation for healthy eating for life.

Some additional benefits to maintaining a diet rich in whole and unrefined foods like whole grains, dark green, yellow and red veggies, legumes, seeds and nuts, is that they contain high concentrations of antioxidant phenolics, fibers, and numerous other phytochemicals that are said to be protective against chronic disease and slow the aging process. So, to get you further into the spirit of things, I created a top five super foods list to add to your diet, so that you are not only the most radiant girl at the ball but, you'll also have the necessary energy to dance the night away.

five "superfoods" that will catapult you to princess power

cacao (chocolate) :: Of course, I had to have this one on the list, as I hope you didn't think I'm the kind of gal who would want to deny you all of life's little food pleasures, did you? What kind of happily ever after is that? Pure cacao, as we're not talking about the sugary, processed milk chocolate bar in the checkout aisle of your local market, is one of the most powerful and delicious foods on the planet. In addition to lifting moods and supporting cardiac health, cacao is known for its ability to ease symptoms of PMS, enhance glucose metabolism, and is said to help prevent colon cancer.

goji berries, acai, and blueberries :: Still unknown to many people, Goji berries are considered to be a "superfood" because they are a complete source of protein as they have all 18 amino acids, as well as super doses of vitamin A, B1, B2, B6, and vitamin E. Goji berries are known to help protect our liver, enhance our immune system, and prevent premature aging.

Acai, which has been increasing in popularity in recent years, is also a complete essential amino acid, with a high quality of fatty acids - similar to olive oil and salmon. These fatty acids are a natural anti-inflammatory, and are essential for behavioral functions, brain performance, and heart health. Blueberries, probably the most common of the three, are full of antioxidants and flavonoids, which can fight against heart disease, cancer, neurological diseases, inflammation, and cellular damage.

kale :: I have to start this recommendation with a confession, as I had experts telling me to eat this for years, and I resisted terribly. Then, one day at a gourmet health food restaurant, I ate kale in a salad, almost on accident, and fell in love. Kale, like many dark leafy greens, is rich in vitamins A, C, and K, as well as iron and calcium. Because of its antioxidant capacities, vitamins, and phytochemicals, kale is attributed to anti-aging benefits, and is said to reduce the risk of certain cancers.

avocado :: Loaded with a combination of critical fatty acids, anti-oxidant phytonutrients, and essential amino acids, avocados are one of the best anti-aging "superfoods" to consume. High in healthy oleic acid, the monounsaturated fat found in avocados is also known to increase fat metabolism, and is rich in the powerful carotenoid anti-oxidants lutein and zeaxanthin, as well as vitamin E.

nuts and seeds :: Boasting high degrees of vitamin E and monounsaturated fats (the good kind), nuts are known to decrease inflammation and can increase brain function and heart health. Nuts and seeds are also rich in Folate, a nutrient that many studies are now showing is essential for proper brain function and known to help individuals who are struggling with issues of depression.

While these are my top five superfoods, for now, there are several other superfoods as well as regular everyday foods that you can consume to maintain vibrant health. For a more complete list of foods that will help you feel like the princess you know you were meant to be, you may want to research the term "SuperFoods" online, as it will no doubt lead you to many more resources for adding high impact foods to your diet.

So, now that you're more aware of some of the things you may want to consider adding to your diet, I also want to bring your attention to my top five foods to avoid, as these are the ones that can do the most damage to your system — no matter how good they taste.

five foods that will have you leaving the ball early

genetically modified foods (gmo's) :: While you may not have been expecting this to make the top of my list, in recent studies from around the world, they have discovered that feeding GMO food products to animals resulted in various cancerous cell growth, damaged immune systems, smaller brains, liver and testicles, partial atrophy, false pregnancies, and other unexplained anomalies. If you're like me, you may be thinking "Yuck', who wants to eat that?" Well, the current challenge with this issue (at least at the time of writing this book) is that many GMO foods are not labeled as such. Therefore, you could just as easily be consuming GMO corn as you are eating regular corn and not know the difference, because the manufacturer and market don't have to label it.

Also, begin reading the labels of some of your longtime favorite brand pre-made foods, as many of them have switched out ingredients over the years to include certain GMOs, and never bothered sharing that information with their consumers. The best way to avoid GMOs all together is to only buy organic produce and proteins.

To learn more about the health risks associated with GMO foods, you can visit The Institute for Responsible Technology: www.responsibletechnology.org

processed foods :: Processing food in and of itself isn't necessarily a bad thing, as cutting, cooking, dehydrating, and boiling are all fairly natural ways in which we process food. However, what about the processed foods you buy at the grocery store? You know, the ones found in pretty, pre-packaged bags and boxes in the middle aisles of the market. Many of these foods have been put through such deviating chemical processes that there is very little real food left in them. The issue with this, besides the fact that consuming these products will cause your body to crave more calories as it looks for the food value it needs to survive, is that these non-foods cost your body a great deal more to digest, absorb, and eliminate than the nutritional value they're worth. These foods, along with any long-term issues they may cause through regular consumption, leave your body feeling depleted and sluggish, causing you to want to go back to the fridge for more empty calories over and over again.

To learn more about the health risks associated with processed foods, you can visit Everyday Health here: www.everydayhealth.com

sugar :: Besides all the empty calories, sugar wreaks havoc on your body; consuming something as small as a soda pop or candy bar can temporarily lower your immune system's ability to ward off unwanted toxins. Sugar also causes inflammation, which isn't necessarily bad, however, over time promotes aging and disease. Additionally, sugar raises your insulin levels, as an influx of sugar into your body has the same predictable result each time, your blood sugar levels sky rocket. Subsequently, your pancreas will release large quantities of insulin in order to do damage control. Done frequently enough over the course of time, and you may find yourself challenged with any number of levels of diabetes.

To learn more about the health risks associated with sugar, you can visit Web MD here: www.webmd.com

canned foods with bpa or bisphenol a :: While there are agencies out there claiming that BPA, an organic compound used as an ingredient to make sealants and plastics, is safe, in 2008 several governments began questioning its safety as a toxic chemical. In 2010, a report from the United States Food and Drug Administration warned of possible hazards to fetuses, infants, and young children, and later that year, Canada became the first country to declare BPA a toxic substance. Used in the lining of cans, the small amounts that can leach into your food have been linked to cancer, reproductive harm, obesity, ADHD, and immune system harm, and is said to have affected 93% of all Americans. So, to decrease your exposure to BPA, drastically reduce the amount foods you consume, specifically those that are acidic, salty, or fatty, because BPA is more likely to leach into these types of foods.

To learn more about BPA, you can visit Breast Cancer Fund here: www.breastcancerfund.org

non-organic dairy :: It's now common knowledge that cows in our country are being injected with a bioengineered growth hormone to boost milk production (known as rGbH, rSbT, or BST). This has been going on since before the turn of the century, and yet, no one bothered to test how safe this chemical compound really was for human consumption. There is an undisputed fact that the bovine growth hormone stimulates the cow's liver to produce another protein hormone-insulin-like growth factor (IGF-1). Research says that if ingested by us orally, IGF-1 in certain dosage levels can be associated with colon tumors and breast tissue tumors. To be fair, there are debates about whether or not humans absorb IGF-1, however because it's just as easy to consume organic milk and dairy products, as they are conveniently located in most major grocery stores, why take chances?

While I'm not making the claim that GMOs, Processed Foods, Sugar, Canned foods with BPA, or Non-Organic dairy are the causes of these various dis-eases - what I will say is that most princesses I know wouldn't want to leave their health to chance. Therefore, I encourage you to do as much research as you are able to do to make sure that you are consuming the best food products to maintain a healthy lifestyle.

> *"Nothing will benefit human health and increase chances for survival of life on earth as much as the evolution to a vegetarian diet."*
>
> *~ Albert Einstein*

Whether you choose to follow a plant-based diet is entirely up to you. However, what I know is that your body and our planet both stand a better chance for healthy survival if we all cut down on the amount of animal food products that any of us consumes. Therefore, I wanted to provide you a basic breakdown of some the various plant-based diets available, as there is no doubt in my mind that pursuing this endeavor will increase your energy, vitality, and have you feeling as pretty as a princess in no time.

vegans :: Maintain a strict plant-based diet. Most vegans also avoid the use of all products tested on animals, as well as animal-derived non-food products.

vegetarians :: Avoid meat and eggs, but consume plant-based foods, milk and milk products like cheese & yogurt.

lacto-ovo vegetarians :: Maintain a plant-based food diet, but in addition to milk and milk products they also consume eggs.

flexitarians or piscetarian :: While flexitarians basically stick with a plant-based diet, they will occasionally consume, or consume in limited quantity, poultry and fish.

raw foodists :: Eat a diet based on unprocessed and uncooked plant foods, such as fresh fruit and vegetables, sprouts, seeds, nuts, grains, beans, nuts, dried fruit, and seaweed. Heating food above 116 degrees Fahrenheit is believed to destroy enzymes in food that can assist in the digestion and absorption of it. Cooking is also thought to diminish the nutritional value and "life force" of food. Typically, to be considered a 'Raw Foodist,' at least 75% of the diet must be living or raw.

So, now that you've discovered, or at least have a better understanding of your current relationship with food, learned some emotional and energetic triggers that cause you to use choose food to pacify your 'less than' feelings in the moment, and have some real world guidelines to make better food choices, the way your relationship with food goes from here is up to you.

Will you do what you've always done, or will you be who you need to create a life of your own design?

The pen is in your hand what's your story about your relationship with food going to be moving forward?

glass slipper insight :: So, just as it is with every great meal, when you prepare and follow the "right" recipe, you achieve your desired result. Now, here's a chance to write your very own recipe for your happily ever after with food. (Write out a believable story about who you want to be in relationship to food from here forward).

_____

_____

_____

_____

_____

one last thought before we move on to the fabulousness of fitness

When you calibrate your energy or beingness, to say one of being a "Princess," your thoughts, beliefs, choices, and actions, not to mention the types and amounts of food you'll be putting into your body, will always recalibrate in order to support the new definition you are claiming yourself to be. ~ M

SESSION THREE

fitness

you carry me through my activities

without so much as a thank you

i depend on you

to pull me through

so, it's time to take better care of you

fitness

If you've already gone through our session on food together, (which I highly recommend you do) then I'm sure you are already beginning to gain a deeper awareness that who we are being and what we believe has a direct effect on the physical experiences we manifest in our world. So, rather than delving back into your childhood, and entire family history to bring up why your programming about fitness is what it is today, I thought being that this is a chapter on it and all, we would begin with a fitness assessment test.

Don't worry, this test isn't a pass or fail proposition, but more of an opportunity to discover just where your current relationship with fitness lies. Because we are all starting from different places in fitness consciousness, I created this session in such a way as to address each level of fitness or general stage to our relationship with fitness.

I've broken them down into these three stages;

- The Acquaintance Stage
- The Friend Stage
- The Intimate Stage

To discover what level your relationship with fitness is, please take the following quiz (no looking ahead at the answers) in order to begin your journey. At the end, you will calculate your score and see which stage best describes your current relationship, and then jump to the section that best reflects your state of being.

Of course, being that we're all a work in progress, I invite you to read all sections of this chapter to discover areas in which you may want to expand your consciousness and/or, perhaps discover parts of yourself that you could be a little gentler with so let's begin!

How would you describe your current level of fitness?
a)   I'm in fabulous condition
b)   I'm okay, I don't really think about it much
c)   I feel I do all the right stuff to stay fit

How often do you exercise in an average week?
a)   5 or more times per week
b)   I exercise when my time or schedule lets me
c)   I workout a few times a week

What's your level of flexibility?
a)   I stretch daily and regularly do yoga
b)   I usually forget to stretch unless my body aches
c)   I sometimes stretch, but I don't follow a regular routine

What's your level of cardio endurance?

a) More than 30 minutes of cardio in each session
b) I sometimes feel winded after more than 10 minutes
c) About 20 to 30 minutes a couple of times a week does me just fine

What do you believe you struggle with most with when it comes to fitness?

a) I exercise regularly but, need a bigger challenge mentally and physically
b) I don't really know how to go about reaching my goals
c) I've seen results, but I'm not quite where I want to be

drum roll please

If you answered mostly "B's" then you are in the acquaintance stage in your relationship with fitness. If you answered mostly "C's" then you are in the friend stage, and if you answered mostly "A's" then you are in the intimate stage.

Like I mentioned earlier, from here, you can either jump to the stage that best describes your current relationship with fitness, or you can start from the beginning, and potentially fill in any gaps that may be missing from your foundation... the choice is up to you.

acquaintance stage

ac·quaint·ance — n : a person with whom one has been in contact but who is not a close friend.

As acquaintances, it's probably fair to say that you and fitness have at least made contact before, maybe even spent some time in your life getting to know one another better, you know, when you felt like it. And while you may be feeling a little overwhelmed, realizing you've been stuck here awhile, the best way I know to shift your mindset towards creating a more intimate relationship with fitness is to remind you that - at any time you choose, you can make the conscious effort to turn an acquaintance into a friend. You know this because each person you have a great relationship with today, first started off as an acquaintance.

That being said, let's begin renewing your relationship with fitness by addressing why you're only allowing yourself to be acquaintances with it in the first place. Part of the reason we keep someone as an acquaintance, not allowing them any further into our world, is because much of who they seem to be is unfamiliar to us. And, as you're no doubt aware, most of us who see life from this perspective are a little more hesitant of wanting to travel down the path not yet known. Therefore, I want to get you started on the path to having a better relationship with fitness by showing you new ways to establish a good rapport with your body, and to assist you in facilitating the process of making fitness a better friend.

hot and heavy romances fizzle out fast

If you're like some of my clients who discover themselves at this stage, you may be feeling a little like, "As soon as I'm done reading this book, I'm gonna run right out and jump right into a high-powered fitness routine." entertaining thoughts such as possibly buying an expensive gym membership and getting a bunch of complicated gear, in order to physically demonstrate your new claim to be fit. And while I'm all about taking action when inspiration hits, I've also noticed that whether it's in two weeks or two months, the majority of people who take this approach seem to fizzle out fast.

This occurs because, when you choose to jump compulsively into situations, you are usually coming from a place that wants to provide instant gratification to your ego. And while serving our ego definitely has its benefits, the typical challenge I see people experience from choosing this path is that they haven't created the foundational support, in terms of their personal beliefs, required to produce their immediate desires.

However, when you're ready to make a lasting transformational commitment, the kind that positively impacts your life in perpetuity, you must begin by laying down a solid foundation of belief. It is from this space of belief that you can create a strong relationship between you and your desired goal, in this instance, fitness.

Therefore, in order to create the best possible circumstances for you to establish a positive, life long relationship with your physical being, I have designed a steady, progressive 'thought-and-action' guideline for your expansion.

Once upon a time, a princess chose to claim a new idea about herself, and as she nurtured this idea, one day at a time, it grew, right into fruition.

If today, the very best you can do towards creating a better relationship with your body is to begin thinking about fitness as much and as fondly as possible, then you are already establishing a better relationship with this aspect of your being. Your intention to connect with your body will start a process where you feel a stronger desire to experience yourself physically. "How?" you ask? Well, every tree that has ever bared fruit began as a seed with the potential of fully expressing the fruit inside it. So too, is the more healthy and fit version of you trying to express itself through your now limited perspective on your physical being.

glass slipper insight :: Whether the process of building a solid relationship with your physical self takes days, weeks, or years, isn't having the ability to fully express your body and health worth it?

wine and dine yourself

When we begin to establish a new relationship with someone, we often put our best foot forward. Whether that's lunching at the local hot spot, or setting up a lovely affair at our home, we try to make a good impression on our new acquaintance. We do this because we believe that by demonstrating care and respect towards our meeting, we are doing our best to create the ideal circumstances from which the relationship can flourish. However, much of the time, when it comes to connecting with our physical body, we're harsh, critical, and sometimes mean and really, who wants to spend time with that version of themselves – I know I don't!

Therefore, when inspiration hits, and you're ready to take action on those fitness thoughts that you've been nurturing, make sure that experience is the best one you can possibly imagine. For example, if a walk feels like the best place for you to start your relationship with fitness, then find an inspirational location for it, turn on your favorite play list, and take some time to notice the amazing nature around you as you move your body. When you're finished with your walk, take some additional time to stretch your body out, acknowledging the stretch in each muscle, and taking a moment of gratitude for your entire performance. When you reflect on your walk throughout the rest of your day, focus only on all the wonderful things you experience. If anything falls short of your desired expectation, make note of it so that you can create an even better fitness experience the next time. The point of this stage of your relationship with fitness is to create as much pleasurable programming around the idea as possible, as this will help you continue to expand upon your relationship.

"Okay, Morgan. I'm in! But, I'm super new to all this. And even though I'm pretty sure I can give more energy to having fitness thoughts, once I'm motivated to do something, I'm not really sure what to do?"

follow the yellow brick road

Because I understand how challenging it can be to start a new relationship with anyone or thing, including our own bodies, I designed a simple path to help you go from the Acquaintance stage to the Friendship stage of your relationship with fitness.

While you are welcome to follow it step by step, my intention with it is to inspire you to discover ways that best help you to deepen, soften, and grow in your relationship with your physical self. No matter how you choose to do it, you have my promise that IF you spend just a little time each day redirecting your thoughts towards being a more fit and healthy you, to the degree that you do, you will experience positive movement in your relationship with your ability to BE fit.

1. Immerse your thought stream in as many ideas for health, fitness, and expressing yourself physically every day, as much as you can.
a) Write affirmations about it.
b) Watch shows or read magazines that advocate for or demonstrate "physical health."
c) Talk to your friends and work colleagues about their fitness routines.
2. Look for signs of inspiration as you continue to nurture this new idea about your relationship with fitness.
a) Notice parks, beaches, and beautiful trails in your area to walk in

b) Look for swimming pools, yoga studios, and fitness centers that look inspiring.
c) Begin to notice more opportunities to express yourself physically in your everyday life – like taking the stairs instead of an elevator.

3. When you take your first steps into physically expressing your new relationship with fitness, be supportive and gentle with yourself.
a) Create whole, beautiful experiences around your first attempts at being physical.
b) Be gentle with your thoughts if your body doesn't perform the way you want it to.
c) Don't put any pressure on yourself to make it a daily thing - just enjoy each experience, and let inspiration guide you into a comfortable routine.

4. Once you begin to develop a fondness for the way you feel about fitness, you may notice that you're beginning to form an attachment.
a) You notice an increase in energy on the days you use your body.
b) You sense that your moods are generally higher when you work out.
c) You feel more confident in other areas of your life

When an activity that you are pursuing, mentally or physically, provides you an experience that feels good to you, you are more apt to continue to pursue it. Therefore, if you make using your body a fun activity, it would be something you looked forward to connecting with, kind of like a familiar friend. Which brings us to the next stage of building an intimate relationship with fitness, or our physical selves - the friendship stage.

friendship stage

friend — n : a person known well to another and regarded with liking, affection, and loyalty.

Aren't friends lovely? They are people we like, know fairly well, and can count on to perform the way we believe they will, most of the time. They're not always perfect, and can sometimes challenge our core beliefs about our being but, at the end of the day, they love us, support us, and reflect back to us perfectly who we are being at any given moment, in relationship to them.

glass slipper insight :: Wait! Are we talking about relationships or fitness? Hmmm. I guess it's so easy to mix up the two since it's all about how we relate to life by who we are being.

in the "friend zone"

When we're in the "friend zone" with fitness, it usually means that we're ranging somewhere between warm, and lukewarm, in the relationship. We may work out regularly for a few months, then taper off to a couple of times a week, or maybe just when we feel like it, only to have the seasons change, which ramps us up again. No matter the current state of your friendship with fitness, because of your long-time intention towards expressing it, the idea of taking care of your body is very well rooted in your belief system.

Because you already have a good association with fitness, my goal in our session together is to help you create an even deeper connection between you and your physical body. With this deeper connection you will be able to experience better physical health, which in turn will make you that much more capable of creating your own happily ever after, and after all, isn't that what this book is all about?

"I get all that Morgan but, what do I do when I don't feel like working out?"

I know. I know. I've been there too. You're on the way home from work and you promised yourself that you were going to take that cycling class tonight but, you really just feel like going home and plopping on the couch for a night of reality television. How do you support the version of you who wants to be more fit?

It starts with a thought

At one point in time, you made a commitment to yourself to experience your body at a greater level than you had before. When you made that commitment, everything in your being did what it needed to do in order to support that idea, to the degree that you believed in it. Your mind, being a part of your energy intelligence system, went into action, doing what the mind does best -

creating as many thoughts as it could think of in order to help you produce that which you say you wanted.

Unfortunately, somewhere along your day you fell into a low mood, and from that lower space, created an internal dilemma by giving yourself a counter command - in this case, "I don't want to work out now, because watching television sounds better." From this new claim, your whole being once again went into action, including your mind, to best create an experience that reflected the new idea. The reason however, you are experiencing a conflict between the two ideas is because the one about you working out has resided within your system longer, and therefore gained deeper roots and a greater desire to be expressed. This is also why all the ideas and thoughts trying to shift you towards going home to watch television have to scream so much louder.

This battle of the thoughts comes about so that you can provide yourself with the best opportunity to make a clear choice. By reflecting upon the potential experience of two opposing choices, you offer yourself the clearest opportunity to declare who you want to be. It's by going through a process of having an experience, and then reflecting upon your feelings about that experience, that allows you to make the best choices to support you on your desired path.

In other words, the power of choice is up to you!

- Do I follow the ideas, thought stream, and energy path that will lead me to my grandest desire, the ability to give full expression to my physical body?

OR

- Do I follow the thought stream and path that will lead me to experience instant gratification in my ego, not having to put forth any effort to attain my long-term goal?

In case the answer isn't obvious, let me spell it out for you:

If you want to experience full physical fitness in your being, you must choose to focus on those thoughts, ideas, actions, and behaviors that help you support the claim you are making for yourself.

mediocrity leads to mistrust

When you have a friendship with someone, you hope that they really give the relationship their all - calling when they say they will and showing up when they make plans. However, in those relationships where the other person has let us down multiple times, and we still like them, we often continue the relationship in a state of less than, or mediocrity. When someone outside of us reflects enough mediocrity back to us in a relationship, we can choose to leave it, in order to leave the experience of it behind us. However, when it is us who demonstrates mediocrity to ourselves, we begin to not trust our own word and commitment to things, which makes reaching our fitness goals even more challenging.

expand the mind to a greater level of awareness + the body has to follow.

In order to get past any mediocre programming, you have given yourself up until now, you must begin to create space for a new trust to be established. When you promise yourself to give it your all, and you don't, you send a clear signal to yourself that you will not live up to your own promises. If you know yourself as someone who doesn't keep your promises, then you must be that much more focused on your state of being in order to assist your mind in creating the highest quality of thoughts available to you.

If you find yourself deep in this space of mistrust, the best way to reinstate your desired level of personal trust is to create regularly attainable goals - the kind of goals that inspire you to complete them and offer you the experience of pride and enjoyment in your accomplishments.

When you better understand the multitude of facets, ideas, and concepts that make up the relationship you have with your physical body - and level of fitness, you can begin to soothe any past hurts (mistrust for not keeping promises to yourself) and address programming issues that need to be up dated with your new understandings.

Because your body cannot express itself physically at a greater capacity than your thoughts are willing to support, you must begin to deepen your relationship with your body - by consistently choosing those thoughts that support your fitness goals.

In order to help re-ignite your passion for fitness, and all the ways it will enhance your world, I created the following 'thought-to-action' guideline.

As with many of my step-by-step guidelines, this information is only meant to be used to inspire you on your path. You are welcome to use it to the letter but, when you make it your own, your consciousness will tend to be much more receptive to it.

how to make the dance a little bit sweeter

1. Create more ideas that support your deepening relationship with fitness.
a) Remind yourself regularly of how amazing you feel during/after a workout.

b)   Acknowledge the physical health you feel as a result of your commitment.

c)   Talk to other people happily involved in healthy fitness routines for inspiration.

2.   Have a reliable dance partner.

a)   Join regular exercise groups / yoga classes.

b)   Hire a Personal Trainer.

c)   Partner up with an equally dedicated friend.

3.   Make sure all the details have been seen to.

a)   Have fun music that inspires you and best suits your activity.

b)   Make sure your exercise clothes and other gear are readily accessible anytime.

c)   Have a backup idea in case your first fitness activity isn't available.

4.   Set aside time to be with yourself physically.

a)   Make this time special by turning off all outside chatter and tuning in to you.

b)   Acknowledge your need for self-care, and make being fit a priority.

c)   Be open! It doesn't matter what exercise you choose, it just has to resonate with you.

When you are in tune with your entire being, mental, emotional, energetic, and physical, your life will be catapulted into a world of your grandest ideas and visions of yourself, and who wouldn't want to be intimate with that?!

And that brings us to our next stage, intimacy!

intimate stage

in·ti·mate — adj : associated in close personal relations; an intimate friend.

As an intimate friend, oh how I know you. I've partaken of your offerings so many times that I almost can't tell where you end, and I begin. My days without you don't feel quite as complete, as thoughts about how wonderful I feel when I'm with you play over and again in my mind. And sometimes, you feel so much a part of me that, if I don't keep my balance, I can lose myself in your world, or sometimes take you for granted in mine. We have a certain ebb and flow, you and I, expanding and contracting with ease, and sometimes grace. And as much as I feel I know and adore you, I also am beginning to realize, we've only scratched the tip of the iceberg.

glass slipper insight :: I believe it was Aristotle that said, "The more you know, the more you know you don't know," and I believe that this idea applies to how well we know our bodies too.

I believe I "knew" my body best when I was around 15 years old, simultaneously swimming for a private league and school team. During that time in my relationship with my body, I had learned a lot about my athletic abilities through a process of physical experience and reflection - things like when and how to push myself, and when it was just time to coast. However, what I understand today, that I couldn't possibly then, is that I had just begun to understand how my entire being really works.

When we're young, all we can see about ourselves is the physical body - how it looks, what parts of us are growing at what rate, and how we manage all its many evolving functions as we navigate the earthly plane. It takes years, if not a lifetime, to truly understand the complexities of what makes it perform in the ways that it does. For me, after personally experiencing every level of fitness described here more than once along with my friends, colleagues, and clients, I have found that the best way to make the greatest physical gains, no matter what your level of fitness, is to listen carefully to your body, following its guidance, and performing your "game" with your entire being in alignment.

where you feel pain, there is wisdom to be gained

Yes, no matter how inconvenient or uncomfortable it may seem at the time, pain is a gift in grace. For when pain shows up in our body, it's a sign that we've held on to a particular belief or thought about ourselves for so long that our energy has manifested it in our physical being. When you feel pain in your body, in order to honor yourself, you must be still and listen to what the pain is trying to tell you.

"Alright Morgan, then what is this "No Pain, No Gain" stuff I've been hearing about my whole life? I thought I had to push myself harder through the pain if I wanted to get results."

Yay! So glad you brought that up.

First off, buying into this particular concept is a sign that you are heavily identifying with your ego. You know, that part of you that wants instant gratification at ALL COSTS. Your ego doesn't care if you're just getting over a cough, it wants to prove it can still drive you through a two-hour cardio class. Your ego also doesn't care if you sprained your ankle right before the local 5K race, as it's going to feed you huge emotionally charged thoughts to provoke you into pushing yourself towards the glory of the finish line.

glass slipper insight :: If you had a friend who tried to force you to workout when you were in a less than capacity, and you knew that you really weren't up to it, wouldn't you tell them nicely to back off? Well, that's exactly what you need to do when your ego is pushing you past your authentic limits.

If dealing with your ego feels a little frustrating, perhaps getting to a clearer understanding of how it's meant to serve you will assist you in better using it.

Your ego's identity is wrapped up in your human-beingness, not your spiritual aspect. Its primary function is to feed you the thoughts and ideas that will best help you experience your separateness from others. This feeling of separateness is vital to your ability to experience meaningful reflection when you come up against various ideas, people, places, or things. It's the part of you that pushes you towards a goal that will make you feel 'special,' and creates the type of thinking that can provoke temper tantrums in fear when you don't find ways to validate it. A better way to understand how your ego comes into play here may be by relating it to a child who isn't getting her own way. You need to take time to explain to her (you), that as soon as you're able, you will put forth the effort to "win-the-race".

So, now that we've temporarily satisfied your ego, let's take a moment to find out what that pain is really trying to tell you. Well, nothing we experience in our bodies or the world is happening "out there."

The concept of "out there" that we're experiencing, in this instance our physical body, is actually part of a greater bio-mechanical feedback system. It is constantly letting us know who we are being by reflecting back to us our chosen beliefs through our physical experiences. The grace being offered when we experience pain comes to us as clues or insights to help us make choices that better our lives. Our pain is there to let us know that our thoughts and beliefs are out of alignment with who we say we want to be, while bringing our attention to areas that need to be processed and healed. Therefore, the only way to truly alleviate the pain is to shift our energy and thoughts around what's causing it.

In order to consistently get the best out of your body, you must establish and maintain a certain level of intimacy with it. If you choose to ignore the pain signal that things aren't quite right in your world, you are telling the very mechanism meant to help guide you towards a better, healthier, and happier life, to "Shut Up!" cause you got this. Take this path enough times and you will find that the pain will continue to get bigger until you finally have to pay attention to it.

I don't know about you but, I'm not a big fan of that kind of pain.

We build intimacy with one another by listening, understanding, trusting, and then adding supportive ideas and solutions to each other's thought streams, as well as working together towards common goals. When you establish a clear connection with all parts of your being, and it performs accordingly, you get to experience what most of us call "The Zone!"

feeling the zone

You know that moment; the one where your body is performing on all cylinders, where time stands still, and all parts of your being are aligned with exactly who you want to be? That's right. We're going to discover what gets and keeps you in the zone.

target :: the zone

YOUR THOUGHTS are in complete alignment with your highest belief about yourself and your ability to successfully participate in the experience. They are maintaining at an even, creative flow to keep you inspired towards your goal. No matter the challenge, you know you can count on your thoughts to support you by feeding you whatever ideas you need to stay in your desired experience.

YOUR BODY feels like a well-oiled (human) machine. You've consistently nurtured its physical growth, paying close attention to build a solid foundation at each level before expanding your abilities. Accordingly, your body is able to perfectly execute every command you give it in order to experience your fitness goals to their fullest.

target :: the zone

YOUR EMOTIONS are steady and even. They are equal to feelings of general happiness or contentment, but with a slightly deeper meaning, one that feels akin to your perceived personal worth or value. You are now basking in the emotionally charged energy of doing a job well done and the natural self-esteem that comes with accomplishing these things. There is no sign of dipping because you feel total freedom of choice to express your physical being.

YOUR ENERGY is being felt in abundance. You have unlocked the "secret code" to access this unlimited source and supply that is within you. Running out of steam is not an option. You feel such inspiration in the moment, that you almost believe your shoulder blades are sprouting wings to carry you to the finish line.

glass slipper insight :: Take a moment to go back to re-read "The Zone" box, and look closely at these four aspects of your state of being. While in this context, they apply to your relationship with the body however, if you look closely, you can see where understanding this formula can help you successfully design other aspects of your happily ever after as well.

"Intimacy... listen to my pain... and stay in the zone... got it!

Okay Morgan, kinda got it. I understand what the zone looks and feels like, but, I don't always know what I'm supposed to do to get there when I'm feeling low?"

I understand, as those are the challenges we all face, no matter what stage of the game we're in. Let's put this back into the context of an intimate relationship. Sometimes, when we've been with our partner for a long time, and haven't given ourselves the alone time necessary to refresh, learn new things, and process our life, our relationship suffers. So too can your relationship with fitness suffer when you don't give it the space that it needs to thrive.

When you feel like things are stagnate or that you're just not as motivated as you want to be, rather than doing the same-old-same-old, do anything and everything to be different. Even if your first attempt at 'being different' doesn't produce the results you wanted, by your sheer intention to be inspired by source energy, you will allow space for new inspiration to come in.

In order to help you further deepen your relationship with fitness, I've created a 'thought- to-action' guideline to inspire you to your grandest vision for your body. While you can use it as a step-by-step path, the best way to allow it to sink in is to make it your own.

how to keep the carriage from turning into a pumpkin

1. Getting further into the zone.
    a) Be aware of what your emotional fitness limitations are, then push yourself towards a fitness belief just outside those limits.
    b) Set progressively challenging physical goals, a little out of your comfort zone, so you maintain your body at a sustainable pace.
    c) Take time to visualize or imagine what your next fitness goal looks and feels like, as though you've already accomplished it.

2. Creating innovative and inspirational goals.
    a) If you've been a gym gal, create a list of all the physical activities you've ever wanted to do that don't include going in to a fitness center for a year.
    b) If you're cardio fit and muscle strong, perhaps it's time to delve into yoga or pilates ~ perhaps adding a meditative aspect to your game.

c) Take time to visualize or imagine what your next fitness goal looks and feels like, as though you've already accomplished it.

3. Pay attention to what your body trying to tell you.
    a) Pain is a gift in grace. In order to best understand this gift, you must pay attention to what the pain is trying to tell you, even if all you can think to do is stay still and feel it.
    b) When you feel the body rush of a great workout, relish in it, for this is the type of experience that represents the epitome of physical health.
    c) By paying more attention to your internal signals, you will know when it's time to push and when it's time to give your body rest, in order to come back and perform another day.

4. Staying happy ever after.
    a) Nurture daily thoughts about ways to expand your fitness level.
    b) Create a mental body/health gratitude list of all the ways you're grateful your body
    c) Make total body wellness your main priority, rather than always looking to achieve a certain level of fitness.]

glass slipper insight :: Now, knowing what you know, your new relationship with fitness can be summed up in one story – your own.

Time to write out your fairy tale fitness routine below.

_____
_____
_____
_____
_____
_____
_____
_____
_____
_____

one last thought before we move to the minds of men

Our day doesn't create our mood, our mood creates our day. For example, when your mood is high, going to work out is a piece of cake. When it's low, you can't bear the thought of stepping foot in a gym. Therefore, be gentle with yourself as you take these next few steps into building your relationship with fitness, wherever you are, as you will no doubt have many of moods to swim through before you reach the castle. ~ M

SESSION FOUR

men

while I like to pretend you're my lover and friend,
the reality is you're just my reflection

you are here for me, to reflect back my beliefs
as we explore our abilities to manifest our dreams

the key however, to creating our happily ever after
is knowing that we were already born as one, in spirit

men

Once upon a time, in a land only feasible in your wildest imagination, lived a stunning young woman with flawless skin, lustrous hair, bright eyes, and a perfectly shaped body, with a voice so sweet that even the animals swoon when they heard its melody. Because of an older more fearful entity that wants to control and destroy her, she flees this land to go to some new, exotic location, only to encounter kinder beings than she's ever known, who are now ready to care for her. Then, through some spirit guide who has been sent to keep watch over her, a prince in a local town is notified that she is in danger. Upon hearing of her beauty and the danger she's in, the prince drops everything, risking perils unknown for the kiss that would make her his wife. After conquering whatever domineering energies are keeping them apart, the prince finds and kisses the princess, and they live happily ever after.

Oops, not so much! I guess that's why they call them fairy tales. Don't get me wrong, I do believe in 'happily ever afters', but this just isn't the right kind of story to show us how to get there.

As perhaps the title of the book indicates, I believe that we are all Princess Charming, demonstrating it in the various ways in which we understand ourselves. And since we all received the same repetitive messages about what romantic love should look like from books, music and movies, most of us believed that there was only one way to get to happily ever after, and if we didn't fit that image, it just wasn't going to happen for us. In truth, there are many types of princesses, each of them creating their very own happily ever after.

So then, after coming to this understanding, I felt that it was about time to have some fairy tales that better reflect what it means to be a human princess in a land called earth, with our various levels of consciousness, physical features, intellect, emotional capacities, and varying moods and energy, so that we can better understand how to create our very own fairy tale. I mean, wouldn't a story that more accurately reflected who you really are and how you use your emotional compass to navigate your journey here help you to better process the entire experience of your life?

Great! I thought so too! This is why I summoned the following human princesses to introduce themselves, their dowry (their value), and their prince to you. I do this with the hope that you can see more value in your being, just as you are, and as you continue in your quest into becoming princess charming. I know when you read the title of this chapter you just knew we were going to discuss men, and all their 'interesting idiosyncrasies,' fun, yes, I know. However, we're going to keep the subject matter focused on your being, as any man who shows up on your personal movie screen (a.k.a. your life) is there because you manifested him by way of your beliefs and energy. Therefore, the point of our relationship session together is to assist you in better aligning yourself with the type of princess you want to be, so that you can better manifest your perfect prince charming.

With that said, may I present some more realistic types of princesses, so that you can see how some alternative fairy tales are working.

princess :: it's all about me megan

I have worked hard to make myself what I am today: queen of my world. Growing up in a family where, whether or not we had it, possessing wealth and material comforts were at the center of my Universe. Therefore, I knew from a young age that in order to have the best in life, I needed to be the best in life, and so that's what I became. Today, my businesses are thriving, I've made all the 'right' types of connections, and I receive VIP treatment everywhere I go. A tastemaker in my social circle, I have access to all the must have designer clothes, dine at the finest eateries, keep up with the latest technology, and my home of course, is the envy of most of my friends. My professional portfolio is impressive, to say the least, as I've been planning the details of my life since I was attending a top University. I love my friends and family dearly, and will usually give them whatever they need but, they have to understand that my life and my work comes first, after all – my life is about me.

personal mantra :: "Being and having the best makes me feel valuable, so I'll do what it takes to get it!"

dowry :: Powerful, Energetic, Confident, Self-Centered, Unemotional, Tenacious

her typical prince charming :: I am more of an easy going guy, definitely reaching certain levels of success in my field but, being more of a background personality. I find that while I may have a certain ability to innovate, because I don't want to be in the spotlight, I will often weigh the consequences of vocalizing my ideas, as taking the lead is not my favorite place to be. Though I may not show it as much on the outside, the things I know about run deep. My friends and family often tell me I'm responsible and kind, as I am the one they go to for solace and advice. So, I while may never be a Captain of Industry, I will leave a trail of peace, joy and compassion behind me.

our fairytale :: Because each of us reflects back to the other similar values or ideals, we sense a certain level of comfort in one another's energy. We both strive for excellence, and doing the 'right' thing, which helps us see eye-to-eye when we create our world together. However, what keeps it interesting is the different ways in which we express ourselves when creating that vision. For example, when she gets too caught up in her me, me, me world, it seems to activate his altruistic side, reflecting back to her that there's more to life than her. And for him, when he gets stagnant, or his ambition seems to leave him, she awakens his passion by reminding him to take forward movement on his goals.

why we share a happily ever after :: We share the same goal of living up to a particular standard of excellence, though one of us receives more value from love, and the other, from validity in the achievement of material goals, our drive to be and do our best will connect us to the top.

princess :: people pleaser penelope

Hmmmmm, how do I tell you who I am without offending you? Well, one of my highest values is to be liked, I mean, doesn't everyone? Growing up in a somewhat distant and controlling household, where my parents guilted everyone about how they sacrificed their whole lives for us, I grew up believing that the only way to receive love was to act how the people around me wanted me to. Accordingly, mine is the office where everyone likes to congregate, because I always bring in yummy snacks. It's the same at home -- everyone likes to hang out at my place, because I am the best hostess, always keeping the food and drinks flowing. My phone is always ringing, usually because people want a favor, and they know I'll say "yes", because I don't want anyone mad at me. Sometimes my personal goals and family relationships suffer because I'm always putting the needs of my friends ahead of my own. While I don't always do what I want, the people around me always seem to have a good time, and that is what's important.

personal mantra :: "I like how it feels to be liked, so I'll do what it takes for others to validate me!"

dowry :: Sweet, Amiable, Nurturing, Low Self-Esteem, Organized, Reliable

her typical prince charming :: While I consider myself a nice enough guy, no one is going to take advantage of, or walk on me. I have friends, mostly the guys I've known since I was a kid, and we're a tight knit group, still partying together on the weekends, without the wife or kids of course. While I've got my own business, and make more than enough money, what I cherish the most is being in the position of control. Having the freedom to choose what I want to do, who I want to spend my time with, and how I want to use my money - that is what brings me the most satisfaction in life.

our fairy tale :: As maybe you could tell, we are two sides of the same coin, my princess and me, as we both struggle with the issue of maintaining our personal boundaries. It is from this perspective that we create the ideas for our life story.

For instance, it drives him nuts that she worries so much about offending someone, that she refuses to say "No!" to a request, mainly because the she doesn't have enough time to do things for him. He is so consumed with himself and his needs, that it gives her the opportunity to express this people-pleasing version of herself constantly.

why we share a happily ever after :: We share a misguided view of our personal self-worth, and keeping up appearances or relations within our peer group. He likes to soothe his personal inadequacies by building himself up as being better than what he actually is, in order to feel valuable. And, no matter what she does for herself and others, refuses to see herself as though she's already enough.

princess :: victim victoria

Who I show you I am depends very much upon what time in my life that we meet. In my career, I've created some amazing dream jobs, only to find myself sabotaging them anywhere from a few months to a couple of years later, landing in an hourly job just to pay the bills. Of course, I've got daddy and relationship issues but, growing up in an environment of alcoholism, codependency, divorce, and not much family around, what girl wouldn't? While I've dated some of the most powerful men around, including professional athletes, recording artists, actors, and even a political professional or two, I always end up with the guy who's got a dream but, is going nowhere fast, and after a while, takes his frustrations out on me. I have lots of friends who, while they love me, worry about how badly my latest beau is treating me, and can't figure out why I am not living at my full capacity. While I sometimes realize I've got some fabulous things going for me, for the most part, I believe everyone who's successful is in on some secret without me.

personal mantra :: "Because I see myself as a victim, no matter how good a situation is, I will turn it into an experience that victimizes me!"
dowry :: Creative, Amiable, Low Self-Esteem, Empathetic, Childlike Belief, Fragile

her typical prince charming :: I am sure you have already heard about me
I am everything you've dreamed of, my beautiful lady. Hey, confidence ain't never been a thing for me love

As my boys labeled me "Genius," which fits like a glove
Spittin' game to women, cheating them right under their nose
They hand over their money, and they take off their clothes
Yeah, top of the food chain, is what they call me
A lot of brains, some brawn, and the right amount of crazy
Getting people to do as I choose, ain't nothing but a game
For I take in no consideration, their humility or pain
For if someone wants to play with me, then they can choose
Play how I want to, or get an offer they just can't refuse

our fairy tale :: Can you see what my lady and me reflect in one another, as our personalities go together like a sister and brother... okay, okay, enough with the rhyming stuff!!! Seriously though, my lady is amazing, she's beautiful, talented, and can run circles around me but I would never let her know that. Look, I've already paid my dues, when me and mine struggled in the streets. This young girl who's got the world by the tail comes and offers to give it all to me, and you think I'm gonna turn that down. Are you crazy? Plus, now that she's in my world, she knows what she'll have coming to her if she ever tries to leave. What, you thought she'd have something here to say about me, have you not been paying attention, I'm the one in charge of writing this story.

why we share a happily ever after :: We share the same feelings of unworthiness, fear, and separation. In order to cope with these feelings of inadequacy, he uses anger and violence as a means to feel powerful and worthy. And she usually complies rather easily, for she knows the lengths he'll go to in order to make her do as he wishes, giving her the perfect opportunity to cry 'victim.'

princess :: controlling connie

Hi, my name is Connie, and I like to do things in a very specific way. I usually take on a lot of responsibility, because I know how to get things done, and I don't want to deal with having to go back to fix them in case others do it wrong. Growing up in a house where a man was king of his castle, I watched my mother stand powerless as dad's decision making caused them to lose their home. It was right then and there that I decided no man was ever going to do that to me. Therefore, in my relationships, I will only let a man treat me a certain way - my way, and if he doesn't, I quickly kick him to the curb. I could probably be making more money if I worked for a big corporation, but, then I would have to answer to someone else, and having my own peanut stand has always provided enough for my family. Accordingly, I live my life with a schedule book in one hand and a 'to-do' list in the other, checking things off one after another.

personal mantra :: "Because the only person I know who's never let me down is me, I take control over everything I see!"

dowry :: Responsible, Anxious, Hard Worker, Controlling, Diligent, Unemotional

her typical prince charming :: Stereotypically, though I'm more mature than anyone gives me credit for, as I'm very well educated and quite worldly, I've been compared mostly to Peter Pan, the man who never wanted to grow up. I know I bring the party wherever I go, attracting environments of wine, women, and song, and can make the object of my affection feel so desirable, that the dullness of her world is now vivid with the colors of possibility. Because I'm so likable, while I may sometimes be out of a job, I am never out of friends who will financially support me. I am highly creative, and can help my partner give life to her deepest fantasies, which seems to make her believe that she loves me, even though really, she's not so sure. No matter to me, she is a princess, and if I can step up to the plate, someday I'll make her my queen.

our fairy tale :: So, it may be rather clear to an outsider who wears the pants in this family, as they both reflect back to one another their fears about anxiety and control. It is from having this congruent belief system that they create their blended reality. For instance, she is so afraid that if she doesn't micro-manage every last detail that her world is going to fall apart, always looking for everything that could possibly go wrong. And he can continue his playful and carefree ways because he knows at the end of the day, she'll always step up to the plate and take responsibility for everything.

why we share a happily ever after :: We share complimentary issues around worthiness, control, and taking responsibility. He doesn't like taking control, because he doesn't believe he has what it takes to maintain the day in and day out responsibilities of life. This in turn creates the perfect opportunity for her to give full expression to her need to be in control, for she feels most valuable when she knows exactly what needs to be done.

princess :: single, sex-crazed samantha

I've got a busy life – a good job, a million friends, and opportunities to travel and party with the best of them. While I believe that most men are jerks, I still date regularly, and have had my fair share of relationships and 'friends.' And, while it looks to everyone else that my life is 'really going on,' what no one knows is that I can't stand to be alone. I hate being alone with my thoughts, because every time I am, I think about why I'm not married with children, like my best friends. I guess being used as a punching bag by an angry parent during childhood has definitely had its effects on me. So, in order to fill any void I may feel, I date just about any good-looking guy who throws a wink and smile my way. For instance, my last relationship wasn't so bad – less than six weeks into meeting him, I found out he was an on-again, off-again drug addict and didn't take care of his kid but - he had a decent job and was great in bed, so rather than walk away, we dated - and decided to move in together six months later. Then, much to my dismay, I discovered while the moving van was still full in our driveway that he was sleeping with my ex-roommate. Love Sucks!

personal mantra :: "Because I believe the world is a scary place, instead of seeing friends and connections, I see adversaries and experience friction wherever I go!"

dowry :: Facetious, Apathetic, Wounded, Flirtatious, Sexual, Impetuous

her prince charming :: It's probably no secret that who I am is not as important as who I'm not in this princess's world. I'm generally a good-looking guy, with most of my act together, including a good paying job, knowledge of some interesting subjects, and my boys will vouch for my loyalty seven days a week. However, I'm just not one to buy into the white picket fence and 2.5 kids thing. I may come off kind of narcissistic or crazy in some scenarios but, these women, they think just cause you bed down with them a couple of times you want to put a ring on their finger. I get it, I do. But, all these women and their crazy issues have me running for the hills.

our fairy tale :: I like to think of our story as more of a nasty affair to forget than a fairy tale. Because both of us have been burned in life, we tend to see people as sources of pain and hurt, rather than of joy and love. It is from this belief or fearful perspective that we engage each other in a combative courtship until one of us feels so much fear in reflection to the other, that we sabotage the possibility of taking it any further. We then go on to date more people, trying to get past our own fears but, with each person who fails to meet our expectations, we end up attracting people of lesser quality who tend to make us feel progressively worse.

why we share happily ever after :: The reason she keeps attracting this kind of prince charming is because she constantly sends out mixed signals of wanting intimacy and also being scared of it, to whatever degree she feels it in the moment. Therefore, when she does get into relationships with men, they tend to find various ways to act out their fears, until they have sufficiently scared each other, and one of them leaves for the next wounded partner.

warning, don't ever take anything personally, as you are only ever feeling your own thinking.

As you can see, each of these princesses attracts the kind of prince who finds worth in her dowry, and vice versa. Therefore, while some of these princesses may evoke uncomfortable feelings in your system, I chose them in particular to assist you in further understanding how it is the type of princess you're being that effects the type of prince you'll attract and not the other way around.

the math & science behind meeting your prince

Here's why, and of course it would take me being in our relationships session together to relate love and romance to math but, for all my gals who've asked me to make love a little more logical, I've broken it down into the following equations to make it real clear:

energy equation :: In order for two energies to blend, they must be vibrating at the same frequency. This is true for liquid to join liquid, gas to join gas, and solid to join solid. So when two people are attracted to one another, it's because they are vibrating at the same energetic frequency, which then compels them to connect in relationship to one another.

mathematical equation :: A + B = C, too simple? Okay. The beliefs that we have in our head about ourselves give us a certain level of worth or value, in this instance "A." As we go along in life, water is always seeking its own level (isn't that geometry?), we are constantly looking for those people who accurately reflect our value back to us, in this instance "B," as we somehow know, when put them together, we make "C" or, in my world – YOU + ME = WE!

Hey, you asked, remember.

glass slipper insight :: In order to better see the kind of prince you're attracting (or are already in a relationship with), take a moment to answer the following questions. As it is through these answers that you will better be able to understand why you're attracting your prince.

- What kind of Princess am I?
- What is my Personal Mantra?
- What is the worth of my Dowry?
- What kind of man is/would be my prince?
- Why is/would our fairy tale be a Happily Ever After?

Our value to each other in relationships is to learn, heal, and balance out the ways in which we express our love and fear. In an effort to best help our princesses increase the value of their dowries and the quality of their relationships, I've created the following magical spells which will also help you shift your value, in whichever direction you choose.

So, if you see yourself in one of those princess's fairy tales, or a little bit of each, here are some new ideas for ways of being that will help you begin to alter your course to one closer to your personal desires.

it's all about giving my ego a break

As I stated in previous chapters, our ego is the part of us that believes it is separate from everything else. It is our human identity, in the sense that it is the mechanism within us that shows us the ways in which we are unique, and are able to distinguish ourselves from others. When used properly, it helps drive us to cross the finish line, open the new business, write a book, and generally achieve our goals. However, when we give it power to run our world, we take things personally – like when we're cut off on the freeway, jump into situations that we know are above our head, or try to force a romantic partner to live life according to our wants.

Just like any of the other parts that make up our entire being, our ego is not the enemy, meant to be criticized or tossed into exile but, rather, a part of us that we need to better understand so that we can help it work to our benefit.

Because your ego heavily influences your thought stream and personal beliefs about your being, when you feel low, it is the part of you that will push you with any type of ideas necessary (positive or negative), to believe that you're a winner. When you create physical experiences that reflect your beingness as a winner, and the ego gets a taste of that sweetness, it will pressure you at all costs, many times against your best and highest good, to move forward on an opportunity it believes will make you feel special, as it relishes in feelings of separation and specialness, which is tempting to most all of us, at least some of the time.

If you are currently living a life from the perspective of your ego, chances are you're never satisfied with who you are, what kind of job or business you have, or how amazing your partner is - you always want more. So the key or magic to creating a better relationship with yourself and balancing your world starts by soothing your ego. Wow! I bet you didn't see that one coming, did you? Yes, an over active ego is an ego that is scared that it is never EVER going to feel special again, which of course isn't possible, as the opportunities to feel special, if we're honest, are plenty.

Regardless of your past programming, you can be re-programmed to experience more well-being and happiness in your system, which in turn will increase the quality of your relationship between you and your partner. To begin this process, acknowledge that you are whole and complete in this moment, just as you are, and that there is nothing more that needs to be added to you, or your world, in order for you to experience this moment, and every moment you go through in life. There is no race to win or goal to achieve, other than the ones that you set for yourself. Your life is a process of claiming your state of being, and then experiencing that state in a physical world that only and always reflects those beliefs back to you. It is from each new understanding that you can either choose to continue down the same thought stream or alter your beliefs to create a reality closer to your vision.

tips for healing an overactive ego

- Practice yoga and meditation to connect with your spiritual source and to remind yourself that we are all connected, if by no other means, that we are all made up of the same energy. Through this action, you will cultivate parts of yourself that believe in connection and equality, and that each of us brings something of value to the experience of life.

- Raise your everyday awareness of how you interact with your ego. Take time to get to know it better and the ideas that trigger it to feel insecure, so you can soothe those thoughts, rather than say or do something that you'll regret later.

the first person I need to please is me

While most of us enjoy pleasing the people that we care about by creating opportunities for them to experience joy, love, and happiness, the motivation behind a person who takes on a 'people pleaser' personality is quite different. On the surface, people pleasers seem friendly, courteous, team players, and often organized. However, they are usually this way because of an irrational thought stream filled with ideas such as "I must be liked by everyone," or "They would never like me if they knew who I really was." What I have found to be one of the biggest challenges in people who live their life from this perspective is they can often rationalize their behavior as being altruistic and necessary to helping the lives of those they care about. However, what they may not be consciously aware of is that they are doing this because there is a part of their psyche that wants to please others in order to avoid reactions that they are afraid to experience.

In order to shift from a people pleaser to someone who pleases herself, let's begin by addressing where your pattern first began. The two biggest triggers I have come across in people who are struggling with this trait are training, whether family, religious or cultural, and being taught conditional love by your earliest caregivers. Training usually comes in the form of receiving messages early on that your feelings or needs are not as important as those around you — such as authority figures telling you that you need to put others first, and that your job is to make them happy. Alternatively, you may have received programming from educators, peers, or society at large based on your gender, age, race, or religion, which said you must please those in power around you in order to feel safe. Conditional love has its own set of variables as well but, the predominate theme is usually that you felt like your parents or primary caregivers only loved you when you complied with their desires as a child.

To release this people pleasing pattern, start by identifying those situations or circumstances that trigger you to act and behave in this way, and then ask yourself what it is that you are scared to feel by saying no to a request that you don't want to fill. Do your best to discover the underlying motivations for your compliance, as it is by acknowledging these beliefs that you can heal them. By being aware of the feelings and circumstances that set you off, you can begin to soothe yourself through self-reassurance that your imagined negative outcome is only a story that you're making up in your head.

Once you've learned self-soothing skills to help you decrease your level of fear and anxiety, begin experimenting with asserting your autonomy. As it is with anything we want to become good at, we must start at the beginning and practice. I would advise the setting of regular small goals for you to achieve, in order to raise yourself esteem. For example, the next time your girlfriend, who never calls you for anything but a favor, makes a request, tell her that you're simply unable, and see how she responds. Try standing your ground in a situation where you disagree with someone who is trying to push his or her perspective on you. When you set an intention to increase your self-esteem and to be more self-pleasing, you will recognize that while people may not always like what you say or do when you assert yourself, they will respect you:

And this puts you in an even better situation to manifest your desired experiences.

tips for healing a people pleaser pattern

- Practice being autonomous. While the patterns of people pleasing may run deep, it is only because you've been nurturing them for so long. When they come up, remind yourself that you're just taking care of YOURSELF, and that everything will be okay.

- Ask more often for what YOU want. Just as you are able to understand the wants and needs of others around you, so too will they understand when you vocalize your own wants and needs. While it may feel awkward internally, simply reminding those around you that you are a real person with your own preferences is a big step forward.

just shift a couple of things around and victim becomes victory

When you feel victimized by life, like you just can't seem to get things to ever go your way, it's because of what you believe about yourself and your world. Every single person on planet earth goes through challenges, I don't care if you are a trust fund baby or if you were raised on the streets, at some point in life, everyone is going to face adversity.

Part of the human experience is going through those situations that will provide us with the greatest opportunity to evolve and finely tune our being. The difference however, between those who go through challenges with ease and grace, and those who let their entire world crumble around them, is perception and belief. When you carry a victim mentality, your awareness of all the injustice in the world, or at least the injustices in your life, are magnified seven-fold. This is because that which we are looking for, we are looking with.

Confused? Okay.

Everything we seek in life is for the purpose of reflecting our inner-most beliefs back to us, for life is a self-fulfilling prophecy. And it is from our level of consciousness or perspective that we establish those things that we are going to look for. Therefore, if you find yourself in situations where you are being disrespected, mistreated, and victimized, it is because at the core of your being, you feel less than, and like a victim. This probably means your fairy tale feels more like a nightmare than happily ever after.

So, how do we go about transitioning your nightmare back into a fairytale? We start by identifying the payoffs you receive by being a victim, so that we can discover more positive ways for you to get to experience those feelings. Some of the biggest realizations I've become aware of by working with individuals who struggle with believing they are a victim is that they enjoy the attention and validation they receive when their life is in a state of chaos. Their ego (yep, it's here too!) gets to feel special as other people express care and concern for whatever it is they're going through. Additionally, if we are victims of life, then we don't have to take much responsibility for the results we get. Because even though creating a life of your own design does require some effort, it may feel like an easier choice to not take personal responsibility for your beingness, and just let whatever happens, happen.

In order to break out of the mentality that is currently binding you, you will have to find different ways to feel the payoffs that being a victim provides you. By discovering the result that you are looking to achieve, you can shift who you are being into one of alignment with those desires. A word of caution, when you begin to shift your current thought stream to one filled with uplifting ideas, there may be a part of you that feels emptiness, for you have given a LOT of space in your head to nurturing the ideas you have about how people treat you, which make you feel like you're not worthy of the life you've always dreamed of. When this happens, calmly remind yourself that you are okay, and begin to fill your mind and time with new things that make you feel good about yourself.

One of the best ways I know for people to begin to feel good about themselves is by taking real responsibility for their own lives. When we don't feel like we have some say in what is going on in our world, we feel helpless and like a victim. However, when we make a commitment to accomplish something for ourselves, and then take the necessary action to bring our desired vision into reality, we receive a huge payoff in increased self-confidence and esteem. I promise, even if they are small goals, you will feel so much better about yourself every time you accomplish something worthwhile that this new behavior is one you will come to want to repeat. Additionally, when we accomplish things for ourselves, we create an internal stability and confidence that turns down the volume on our need for external validation. This further deepens our belief in our own abilities, including manifesting a kind and respectful prince charming.

tips for turning victim into victory

- Practice being grateful for the good that is in your life. Whenever you feel like a victim, ask yourself, "Is there someone in the world that may have it worse than me?" It's not that this question provides you the most uplifting of images, however, it can really snap you out of your limited perspective in the moment. Once you lift yourself to this greater perspective, you can begin to ask, "What can I learn from this situation?" for your intention to find the good in it, will usually reveal what drew it to you in the first place.

- Forgive yourself and anyone in your world that you feel did you harm. Begin by acknowledging that the person that did harm to you, or created the experience for you to feel like a victim, was only responding to your unspoken request to do so. For as long as you choose not to forgive that person, they will hold power over you, as thoughts of their 'wrong doings' will take up space in your head until you release them. Additionally, you must forgive yourself for the thoughts and beliefs that you held to be true, which created those experiences, since you were only operating from the level of consciousness you understood at the time.

the only type of control I need is over me

Though it would appear on the surface that a controlling person is rather powerful, individuals who need to exert control over others in their world actually struggle with deep levels of anxiety. They exert their authority in order to avoid feelings of helplessness, and usually believe that they can control others emotionally and physically as a means to feel safe in their world.

Living from such a tense perspective, one may wonder how and why they took on this controlling way of being on in the first place. Typically, though a sudden chaotic life event can trigger controlling behavior, most controlling people first develop this way of being through early childhood programming, as a means of coping with the anxiety they felt in their world. Many had parents or caregivers who weren't able to fully care for them, or somehow needed them to take on adult responsibilities in order to make the household run. Taking on such levels of responsibility at a young age, the person quickly develops a tendency towards feeling pressure, anxiety, and worry, which continues to compound as they go along in life.

As it is with all habitual behaviors, there is a benefit to the person who is being controlling. Because controlling people often receive the validation they crave from effectively demonstrating their controlling behavior, approval can be confused with love. Therefore, we may begin to believe that we have control over making others love us. Accordingly, our controlling behavior towards others comes from our unwillingness to accept that we have no power over others' feelings and being. Paradoxically, realizing that we have no control over the behavior of others, actually leads us to our own personal power.

"But Morgan, if I don't take control of things, how am I ever going to receive love and approval?"

When you make helping and taking over situations your primary relationship skill, you lose the ability to have deep and genuine connections with people. This often occurs because, in order to take control of someone, you have to see him or her as weak or not quite your equal. Over time, rather than love you for your generosity of spirit and ability to handle things, the person you are trying to control will resent you for not allowing them the freedom of expression, including making mistakes, that they need to develop fully as a person in relationship to you. This cycle of needing and resenting plays havoc with your esteem, which typically causes you to want to exert more authority over the relationship. Therefore, as long as you make someone outside of you responsible for your feelings of worth, validity, and love, you will try to control how they treat you. When you accept that the only person you are actually in control of is yourself, then you release yourself from this cycle and allow for a healthy relationship to emerge.

One last thought – as long as you maintain your controlling behavior identity, the only type of people you are going to attract to you, for any amount of time, are those who are fragile, and need you to take care of them. Ironically, the biggest compliant I hear from women who struggle with this very issue, is that the men in their life are weak. Therefore, if you want to attract a stronger prince charming, then you must recognize that strong men want their autonomy, and you must relinquish your dictatorship ideals, in order to rule your kingdom together.

tips for loosening your controlling grip

- Remind yourself that you are helpless over the feelings and behaviors of others, and begin a "no advice" policy with those you love. It will be a challenge to break this cycle however, being conscious of it is the first step.

- In those times where you offer unsolicited advice, take a moment to apologize to the person whose boundaries you've crossed, as this can go a long way to maintaining the relationships you have with those you love in your life.

from single to mingle, when life's not so scary

Dealing with issues of intimacy are challenging, even for the most well balanced of us, as there is always an associated risk of rejection when revealing ourselves to others. Often times, individuals who struggle with intimacy issues don't even realize that they have them, as their lives can be so filled with people, friendships, and sometimes even committed relationships, that they don't necessarily make the association that intimacy issues are the reason why they can't seem to find themselves in a supportive and loving relationship.

Most everyone wants and needs to experience intimacy, to some degree, yet the very process of creating intimacy can be filled with angst and disappointment. As it is with everything we experience, the root of our issue with intimacy is not external, in that we can't find the right person to be with, but rather, is an internal issue wherein we haven't come to fully and unconditionally love and accept ourselves. Somewhere along our life path, we accepted certain programming from outside sources that whoever we really were wasn't good enough to be accepted. Typical programming for these ideas usually stems from a disapproving caregiver, authority figure, or rejection from your peer groups in school. However, there is a light at the end of this tunnel, as these limiting ideas you hold about yourself can be transformed in such a way that you can comfortably share yourself with others in an intimate relationship.

Because feelings of inadequacy are usually our reason for interacting with others in a superficial mode, in order to help create more intimate relationships, you must first develop a better relationship with yourself. Developing this better relationship with yourself occurs through a process of discovering who you really are, which increases yourself worth as you come to better value your being. This exercise will serve as the foundation for allowing you to share your authentic self with others. Also, communication is key to creating closeness in a relationship, so by practicing your communication skills, you will feel more solid when communicating intimate ideas about yourself to others.

"But, I don't want to put myself out there like that. I'm happy having a bunch of superficial associations that keep me busy, that's the whole reason I operate this way."

I know that's what you tell yourself but, I'm going to be a little bit in your face and tell you the reason that you don't want to put yourself out there like that isn't because you're happy operating this way, it's because you're scared. Whether you've created stories in your head that intimacy is too hard, smothering, or that everyone around you is a 'jerk' and that's why you don't go deep with them, you've repeated these ideas over and again to support you in your belief that you need to protect yourself from the rejection of others. So, while you may be a very busy gal, I would also assume that any moment that isn't filled to the brim with things to do and people to see, leaves you feeling lonely and empty.

In order to keep you from scaring yourself as you begin navigating these deeper waters of intimacy, take baby steps from the shallow end by getting progressively closer to friends with whom you already feel a connection. Intimacy isn't something that happens in one night of passion with someone, it is something that evolves over time, through a building of trust and shared experiences. Therefore, in order to feel true intimacy with another, you must practice revealing yourself to them slowly, like peeling back the layers of an onion, one at a time.

When you take the time to get to know and love yourself more fully, you will begin to understand how much you contribute and are valuable to others - by being your most authentic self. When you demonstrate this value through way of your being, you will attract an authentic prince, one waiting to create an intimate happily ever after.

tips for increasing your level of intimacy

- Spend time getting to know yourself in a more intimate way, discovering those parts of yourself that are easiest to share with another, and those that you need to develop more self-acceptance of - so as to soothe yourself from any feelings of unworthiness in relationship to another.

- Practice being intimate with people who are already familiar to you. Take baby steps in building trust by sharing quiet and uninterrupted time with that person that you are looking to be more intimate with. This may include; quality conversation, expressing your feelings through words and actions, sharing the details of your day, and being able to listen to them with care and understanding.

every man you meet is a prince charming

"Okay Morgan, I've given you lots of leeway with some of these new and unusual ideas so far but, there is no way you're going to convince me that every guy I've been with was a prince. You have no idea about some of the — ahem 'stuff' that I've been through."

I know, and I feel your hurt and pain but, I promise you, each one of those men who didn't treat you the way you believed he should have, provided you the opportunity to declare yourself as being so much more than what the situation was offering you and with that, the gift they gave you was priceless.

Each man you have ever chosen to be in a relationship with was reflecting back to you who you believed you were in the moment. Nothing more. Nothing less. If a man is supportive, caring, kind, and compassionate, look within and you will see where you are demonstrating your belief of these qualities in yourself. If a man is abusing you, constantly saying mean things and creating a general atmosphere of anxiety, fear, and pain, then look within to see where you are lacking internal compassion for yourself and your being; thereby, calling in the experience to be abused.

what happens when I meet my prince charming, and then blow it?

A couple of years back, I met an amazing woman. She was striking to say the least - tall, beautiful, intelligent, and when she smiled, she could light up the room. So, when she started sharing with me about her man problems, I was caught slightly off guard, at first. She was a little over five years out of a domestic violent relationship, wherein she had been verbally, emotionally, financially, sexually, and physically abused, and outside of a couple of dates, had been single the whole time. However, a few of months prior to coming to see me, she had met the first man that made her 'sparkle' in over ten years.

They met on a work project, both sensing an instant chemistry. During the project they would flirt and drop little hints of interest to each other but, because of the nature of the project, they couldn't yet pursue a romantic relationship. So, over the course of many weeks, they became more and more friendly, and the friendlier they became, the more she fantasized about the potential of what dating him would be like. They had so much in common, everything from their careers and being single parents to the sport they played in high school and where they chose to live. She just knew he was the one she had been waiting for to take her out of her self-imposed exile from relationships.

When there was a lull in the project, he invited her to a party he was throwing for some of his work colleagues and friends. Though elated by the offer, rather than being excited to be with him outside of their work environment, she began a thought-stream that established all the reasons he didn't like her, wouldn't like her, and if he knew all that she really was at that moment, wouldn't want her. She built up this story of negativity, which she played right up until she opened the door to the venue of the party.

Of course, when she arrived, he made her feel special and welcomed, introducing her to all his friends. She was thrilled to be there, however, when he had to go back to entertaining his guests, all the programming of unworthiness that she had been playing over and again in her head, came out to express itself in full force. According to her, she didn't do or say anything to embarrass herself, however, after a time of being there and not understanding all the players at the party, or her role there, she let her overwhelmed feelings take over and tried to leave without saying goodbye. She told me he called after to her as she was leaving but, because of the tears already starting to stream down her face, she wouldn't turn around to give him any opportunity to soothe her. So, she went home, crying the whole way.

When they resumed their work project, he was still very nice to her but, the damage had been done. While her ego tried to ignore what had been broken, he was not in the mind space to rescue her from whatever had caused that situation in the first place. Probably needless to say, he went on to find someone who was in resonance with his happy, high vibrating frequency, and she now found herself sitting with me, trying to make sense of how and why she behaved this way when he was exactly what she wanted.

Have you ever experienced a situation like this? Maybe not this exact one but, one in which you met someone who just seems to rock your world, and instead of being who you needed to be in order to manifest the experience, you self-sabotaged with feelings of unworthiness? Well, I'll start by offering you my condolences, as this is usually not a pleasurable experience for any of us to go through. However, this is a book about becoming princess charming, and so I will share with you, what I shared with her so that she could better learn from her experience, and how to apply the lesson to her bigger vision of happily ever after.

In order to first soothe her feelings of pain and separation, I reminded her that it was who she was being which attracted him to her in the first place, and how fabulous it was that she had gone from being someone who attracted an abusive person, to now attracting someone who was successful, handsome, had great energy, and was kind. I congratulated her on how much she must have expanded her consciousness in the last five years since she left the abusive relationship to find herself face-to-face with such an amazing person who was in fact, reflecting back to her the person that she was now revealing herself to be.

To further shift her perception of the situation into one that would really work for her, I invited her to change the way she looked at things. Rather than seeing him as 'the-one-who- got-away,' she could choose to look at him as the sign of what's to come. Often times, when we're making breakthroughs in our states of being, we'll get little glimpses of what we're creating, like when we witness the first green stem of a fruit tree breaking through the dirt. The green stem isn't the fruit but, it is a sign that the process of evolving and fruition are taking place, and left uninterrupted, will go on to bear fruit.

Of course, like most of us, she wanted what she wanted in the moment. But, once we got a few months past the situation, and her self-perception continued to evolve, she realized that, while he was amazing, perhaps his lifestyle wasn't what she wanted after all. And that had she gone down that particular road, she might not have made the growth necessary to become the princess charming she is today.

glass slipper insight :: If this is where you find yourself in your fairy tale, remind yourself that the mere fact that a Prince you actually liked showed up in your world, is a sign that you're beginning to believe in his existence.

"I'm stuck with a toad - how many times do I have to kiss him before he becomes a prince?"

tips for preparing yourself to meet your prince charming

Write a list of all of the qualities you are looking for in a partner, as these are the qualities you most want to experience in yourself.

Once you've identified these qualities, begin to demonstrate them to yourself, in any positive way you can.

Begin to feel now, how you believe you will feel when you are in relationship to your prince.

Increase your awareness of those parts of you that are resistant and fearful to being in an intimate relationship - and begin to heal them.

Well, with a question like that, I know we've read some of the same fairy tales. I hate to break it to you but, no man in this reality is really a toad, unless that's the way you choose to see him. As I'm sure you're already beginning to grasp, there is nothing outside of us that shows up in our world unless we believe it to be true.

Therefore, if your guy looks more like a bumpy, green amphibian than a knight in shining armor, perhaps rather than trying another magic kissing spell, we need to get you to a more enchanting perspective.

The day that you and your prince said "I do" to whatever kind of committed relationship you're in, it was because you shared a similar vision for your partnership and lives that resonated between you. However, often times as we evolve in life, we don't always do it in such a way that is completely congruent between our partner and us. This occurs because, as I'm sure you can attest, while it can be challenging enough to balance and maintain the ideas, beliefs, and experiences that come from just your dreams, fears, and ambitions, bringing two ways of being together can be twice as hard.

Many times, when a relationship begins to derail, or you believe your prince has become a toad, it's because one of you began to focus on and give energy to an idea, or series of ideas, that detracted from the original vision for your 'happily ever after'. While a few ideas alone aren't usually enough to throw the whole connection off track, they are definitely enough to start creating a 'bumpy ride'! So, when these thoughts and ideas, along with the others that will inevitably form to support your growing beliefs, begin to permeate your thought stream, you tend to no longer give your partner the love, validation, appreciation, or even respect he deserves.

Because your partner can feel your building rejection, even if it's only on a subconscious level, they will usually respond by either building up a steady stream of resentment towards you, being flippant, snappy, or demonstrating an inconsiderate attitude, to match your now less than loving energy. Alternatively, if being happy is their priority, they will find other means to pursue their happiness that take them emotionally and energetically away from your relationship. This can also happen on both sides, where each of you feels unseen, unloved, under-valued, or just plain taken for granted. Now, you're both going to look outside the relationship to find other ways to fulfill your needs. Obviously, this is the type of scenario that tends to break the relationship completely apart and pushes you to find your happily ever after with some other prince.

Provided that no one is abusing anyone and that there is still love and growth to be experienced between you and your guy, the best way to begin to turn that toad back into a prince is by staying in tune with both you and your partner's current perspective or being. As it is with this intention and awareness that you will create a stronger desire to stay clear on who you are as a couple and what you want to experience in your happily ever after.

"Okay Morgan, I understand what you're saying, but I already have a pretty strong resentment going towards my partner and I don't know if I really care who he's being right now."

I understand that, and while I have sympathy for the pain you're currently feeling, I must remind you that you were a full participant in how your relationship got to the place it is now. Remember, it was who you were claiming to be in reflection to your partner; how you interpreted his words, moods, actions, and behaviors, that caused you to judge him as being something other than what you wanted to experience at the time. And, the more that you focused on all the ways that he was letting you down, the bigger all of those parts of his being began reflecting themselves back to you.

The good news here is this, any experience that thought and belief has gotten you into, it can get you out of which is exactly how we're going to turn your frog back into a prince.

To begin, you must remind yourself of all of your partner's amazing qualities and yes, he's still got them under all those slimy green scales! You just have to shift your focus on to those qualities, so that they are the things that are reflected back to you most. More than just a lofty thought or affirmation you've heard before, it's so very true, what we focus on grows. This is because the more focus you give something, the less focus you are giving to other things. Therefore, the thing you are focusing on most seems to be what's biggest in your world.

In order to receive love, care, consideration, kindness, sexual attraction, and fun, you must put forth the belief and demonstrate those qualities within yourself first. You must nurture the thoughts, ideas, and beliefs that keep you connected and inspire mutual love and respect. Then communicate those ideals to your partner so that you can collectively create a life that fulfills you both and helps you see him as the knight in shining armor that he was when you first fell in love. Isn't that what happily ever is all about?

turn your toad into a prince

Wipe the slate clean -- forgive yourself and him for letting the relationship get to a place that doesn't fit either of your visions for happily ever after.

For 30 Days--in a row--write a list of the top 20 things that you love about your partner.

Make plans to go on at least 4 dates during these 30 days – each date, dress like a princess, flirt & ask him first date type questions that will you allow you to better see who he is currently being.

Begin to act now as though your relationship already forming the ideal happy ending -- and then enjoy how it all unfolds for you.

glass slipper insight :: Okay, it's your turn. You've read the fairy tales, where you now believe they got it right and maybe a little wrong, and how you can consciously create your own.

Write your new romantic fairy tale, one full of love, passion, kindness, consideration, and you. Let your imagination pull in all sorts of scenarios that will bring happiness to your world and write a story you can believe in for it is your very belief in it that makes it come true.

_____
_____
_____
_____
_____
_____
_____
_____
_____
_____

one last thing before we move on to the mountains of money

Don't take anything that anyone does personally, as you are only ever responding to your own thinking. The best way to stay on your path to happily ever after is to remember that all we are ever feeling about are the thoughts going on in our head. If we are thinking sad, low, or depressing thoughts, we will feel bad. If we are thinking productive, happy, and passionate thoughts, we will feel good. Therefore,

anytime your romantic partner does something that makes you feel happy or upset, remind yourself that it wasn't what they did that you're responding to... but, what you think about what they did that gets you every time.

When you get this, you will have the magic you need to make every day feel like you're becoming princess charming.

~ M

SESSION FIVE

money

you must demonstrate your value,

so that you can feel your worth

money

Money is the easiest thing in the world to manifest

Do you believe that is a true or false statement?

Hmmm..... interesting answer. Now, what if I said that whether you believed it was true or false totally depended upon your perspective, and not whether in fact money is easy or hard to attain. How would you feel about that?

During the course of my work and life, I have had the honor and pleasure of coming to understand the consciousness and energy of many cultures and subcultures - being with different types of people so intimately that I learned to live among them in their personal environments in harmonious community. I have dined on fabulous food in the finest of restaurants, played at the best hotels and entertainment destinations, worn designer clothes, shoes and hand bags, driven luxury automobiles, and partied with people so famous for their craft that you would know their names instantly if you were familiar with their chosen field. Equally, if not more character and compassion building, are the chapters of my life wherein I experienced up close and personal the lives of drug dealers, pimps, Hollywood and music industry wannabe's, strippers and prostitutes, and those so desperate for material goods that they would place their grandmother's, mother's or even child's good name on the line for money, even when they knew there was a good chance, they weren't going to pay it back.

Because of each act I've witnessed, each conversation I've engaged in, and every experience I've taken part in up until now, I know with the utmost certainty that the way you experience money in your life is in direct relation to the value you place upon it and who you believe you are in relationship to that value.

so, what do you believe money is

Before you can create something in your world, you must first understand how you define it, and what value or worth you assign to it in your belief system. The value of any particular thing is always a perceived value by the observer of the object, as there is no absolute value of any object, for value can only be perceived by the person in relationship to it. For instance, I have an acquaintance who loves, loves, LOVES jewelry, especially diamonds. Every time her husband gives her a new piece of jewelry, she tends to show it off, tell everyone where he got it, and sometimes it's retail value. Now, don't hate me but, I could almost care less about 'real' jewelry – I said almost! I just don't place a premium value on producing it in my life experience. Therefore, if she and I were presented a certain challenge in order to receive a piece of fine jewelry, who do you believe would be more motivated to complete the task? She would. Yes, exactly! The person who places the most value on the perceived prize is always going to be more motivated than the person who places less value on the end result or experience, in this case, jewelry.

I chose the above example, so you could clearly see two different perspectives on something that most of us place at least some value on, jewelry, as our very culture programs us to believe that the monetary value of the item someone gives us dictates how much they love us. But, we'll get more into your programming about money later in the session. For now, the reason I bring this up is because when you understand that everything in your life, including money, only holds the value in your world that you place upon it, it positions you into an expanded state of awareness wherein you are able to see why you experience money in the ways that you do. If you believe that money is a coveted and limited resource, one in which your survival depends on, you may find it much more challenging to experience it at the levels you desire. However, if you believe that money is nothing more than a symbol or means of exchange for you to get the things that you need to enhance your life experience, then you may not place as much of a premium in coveting it, and hence find the demonstrating of it in your world to be rather easy.

Now, you may be saying to yourself "I know I place the 'right' value on money, and I know I work hard to get it, so why then am I not making the kind of money I believe I deserve?" which is a completely valid view point, and one that may appeal to a basic common sense perspective. However, I am asking you to dig a little deeper, as our relationship with money, just like any other relationship we have, has multiple facets to it, which influences the way we believe about it, and how we work towards creating it in our world. To help you begin to further examine your beliefs about money, I invite you to read through the following ideas about it, so that you may gauge your emotional responses to each. Please note, there are no correct answers or insights to be had in this exercise, as we are only trying to discover where you currently are, so that you may build the type of relationship with money that better supports your desired reality.

glass slipper insight :: Ask yourself, "Who am I in relationship to this idea about money?" as you read through each of the ideas below. Take note as to any thoughts, beliefs, or emotional sensations that come up as you do, for these feelings are there to offer you insights as to your current belief system and relationship with money.

1. I believe that all my problems would be solved if I had more money.
2. Only people who are have no integrity get rich.
3. Money is a tool, as it allows me to buy the things, I need to make my life work.
4. I feel like I shouldn't charge much money for what I do, as I'm blessed to do it
5. I work hard for a living and believe I deserve every dollar I earn.
6. I love money, the more I have the better I feel about myself and my life.

When you read those statements, what came up for you? Did you laugh or get angry? Did you resonate with any of the ideas, maybe a few of them from different perspectives you've had in your life? Whatever it is that came up for you, the point of this exercise was to further draw your attention to that fact that any perspective you hold about what money is what sets the foundation for how you go about creating your entire relationship with it, and hence your ability to experience it in your world.

For example, if you believe that money is unclean or evil, and you believe that you are a clean and good person, then because your beliefs about who you are stand in direct contrast to what you believe money is, you create a block in your ability to receive it - no matter how hard you work to get it! If your energy isn't equal to or in resonance with the thing that you desire, in this case money, you will not experience it in your physical reality. This is because your reality is nothing more than your beliefs being reflected back to you through your physical experiences. Think of it this way, if I believe I'm clean and I think money is dirty, by way of my combined belief system on the subject I will block money from coming to me, rather than welcoming it, as ideas of good and evil are repellents to one another. Accordingly, in order to experience money at the level you desire, you must first have an internal belief system that supports that desire.

To help you further understand how various beliefs about money are experienced in this physical reality, I found three human princesses who are living their own happily ever after fairy tales and are willing to give you a sneak peek into what life is like in their kingdom and castle. What I want to remind you of as you read their stories, is that each princess can only create a reality that she understands and believes in, by way of her consciousness. To be clear, it's not that any kingdom or castle described here is any better than another, for each has a significant purpose to serve for the princess who is creating it. In essence, each kingdom being created is being done in such a way wherein the princess creating it can see what her internal beliefs about who she is reflected back to her in an external world. For it is only through her experience that she can see where her beliefs serve her in creating a happily ever after, and where perhaps she needs to rethink her ideas in order to create a better result.

the life of the pauper princess & her palace ::

Most days when I wake up, the first thoughts that cross my mind are about work, how I'm going to pay the bills, and feed my family. Often tired and a little achy from working so much without making the progress I desire, I can sometimes be a bit snappy with my loved ones who request things from me, fearful that I will never have all the resources to live life how I want to be. Because I frequently seem to be a little short on cash some people think I'm lazy, however, they have no idea how much I struggle and slave each and every day, just to make it through. Sometimes, I wish there was a way out of this life I've created, some magic pill I could take that would transport me to a real happily ever after, you know?! The kind we read about as little girls. I have big goals, if people only knew how many amazing ideas I have to achieve success, if only I got the chance to do them. But I'm so caught up in my daily grind and the little money that it affords me, that I don't believe I'll ever have time to pursue my dreams.

My cute Craftsman style palace may not be a show piece however, despite the outdated plumbing and stains on the carpet, this charming little home still belongs to me. As for entertainment, all we've got is an old television and Netflix on repeat, yet no one complains about the picture being less than perfect, as we all huddle on top of one another on our cozy living room couch, just so we can be together. While there are many things around the place that could use my attention or at least a simple upgrade, my biggest frustration comes from the fact that whenever I am able to get the resources together to do something nice, like purchase a new piece of furniture or technology, something like having to get a leaky pipe fixed or removing the bees from plugging up my chimney has to be taken care of first. Everyday seems like I'm constantly having to swim upstream.

Don't get me wrong, my kingdom isn't always full of such frustration, as there are the times, I'm riding high, or at least sliding right through what could otherwise be disastrous situations, getting little breaks here and there when a client or the boss decides to actually pay me what I'm worth, or a barter or trade comes in to save the day. And, while I am grateful for these little mercies, living this way on a constant basis is highly taxing and stressful, as I never seem to get a break from feeling like I'm just one or two moves from being banished from the castle.

what my life says about my beliefs about money :: Though I experience it at differing degrees, depending on what's going on around me, I definitely resonate with a poverty mindset. This is not to say that I am necessarily poor but, more specifically that I hold a mindset that is congruent with ideas that life is an upward struggle, filled with lack and limitation. The type of thoughts that permeate my mind about creating wealth may look something like "You have to work hard or be born into the 'right' kind of family to be wealthy." or "Only lucky people get breaks, the rest of us have to struggle to make it by." The successful people around me often get frustrated with my inability to create my visions, or as it's been fed back to me, all my "false starts," believing I don't have enough initiative or that I'm too sensitive to ever achieve my dreams. However, what they don't understand is that I'm always making forward movement, creating my reality from the perspective in which I am able to see. My challenge is this: what I believe most is that I am subject to the whims of life, and whatever destiny may have for me. Therefore, even in those times that I do experience a proverbial windfall, because I identify with lack, I don't have the belief system in place to support my ability to keep my money and use it wisely.

the life of the material girl & her mansion :: When I awaken in the morning, the first type of things that cross my mind are about the people I have to play nice with that day because I have business dealings going on with them, and the vendors I'm going to have to yell at for not keeping my manufacturing costs down. No sooner do I start my morning workout, before I receive a barrage of employee emails and text messages, clamoring for my attention in order for this, that, or the other thing to be accomplished. Because I'm constantly having to be on top of my game, people often treat me like I'm a bit of a machine, able to respond to anything in a moment's notice. However, what they don't know is how much I've suppressed my emotions in order to be able to operate like this, and how much the stress is killing me. If only they knew how much I sacrifice in order to have this kind of life, if only I could take some time off to explore who I am and what I'd like to believe. However, if I take my eyes off the goal for even a moment, my world will come tumbling down around me.

With tall ivory towers and fresh bougainvillea growing up the side, my mansion is fashioned like an Italian Villa, designed by the finest architect's mot du jour, and furnished with one-of-a-kind collectables from around the world, but isn't filled with much family. Featured in some of the finest home and garden magazines, and used as a regular venue for society parties, my house often feels more like a museum than home sweet home. Even when I want to be alone, just to walk to the fridge in my t-shirt and undies, I have to be concerned one of the many employees I need around to help maintain my world might spot me. Sure, I make the money I need to support all this but, what frustrates me is that everyone around me thinks of my place as an entertainment destination, rather than a serene place I use to call home. Of course, it's great to have money but, sometimes it feels like the only thing I'm good for to anyone is earning it, as no one seems to care about getting to know the real me.

I don't want you to think I'm indulging in a pity-party, as I know I've got it good. I get to dine where I want and buy all the latest designer goods a girl could ever ask for. I understand that I have access to all the resources that money can buy, as there is no debating that however, living in a fish bowl where the only reason anyone loves or respects you is because of how much money you're making them is very isolating, as it often feels like if you don't make their money quota, you'll be removed from the very kingdom you built.

what my life says about my beliefs about money :: Since I can remember, I've had more than enough money to buy the average person's lifestyle three times over. This isn't to say that I have so much money that I'm out of touch with reality. More so, I have come to believe in a life wherein money is king, and almost everything I do is to attain more of it. Because I identify almost my entire worth on how many digits are included in my bank balance, I am often filled with thoughts such as "If I don't make enough money or have the things that my friends have, then I am nothing" or "Because I'm so rich, the only reason anybody thinks to spend any time with me is because I make money." The people who come around me, often do so because they believe hanging around me will make them successful or have more money. However, I do notice no one ever asks me about the sensitive or compassionate things. What no one understands when they see me living this way is that I create this reality because of what I believe about money and the ways it can validate me. The challenge with this belief system is that I identify my personal worth and ability to receive respect from others based on the amount of money I am making. Therefore, even though it doesn't seem like I have money issues, in fact, much of my very ability to feel loved by others, and myself, is linked to how much money or success I have at a particular time. The sad truth of the matter is this; even when I do meet someone who doesn't love me for my money, because I'm so caught up in it as my primary identity, I can't really experience them with any genuine intimacy.

the life of the balanced princess & her beachside condo ::

I wake up every morning excited about life and thinking about the project I am going to get to work on that day. Knowing that I'm going to get to express my creativity soon, as part of my morning routine, I quietly sit in front of my computer addressing any messages that require my attention from the day before. Because I do what I love for a living, my work doesn't stress me out, or if it does, it's usually because it's time for me to grow to the next level, and that means time to step out of my comfort zone. My days are often busy but, because of the way I've structured my life and business, I am able to show up as a professional, a lover, a mother, and a friend all in the same day, usually without skipping a beat. Because money isn't what drives me in my world, not everyone always understands my motives. Sometimes, I turn down what may look like a lucrative deal in order to maintain peace and balance in my world, and while that may mean I miss out on a certain vacation or have to delay remodeling the kitchen for few months, I know that because I didn't create stress and chaos around me, another opportunity that's better for me will soon come my way.

My Mid-Century Modern ocean-view condo offers me the best in simplicity and luxury. Because I like to live within my means, I chose a modest place by the water because location is everything to me. Each morning, I walk out onto my patio to gaze at the ocean, for just being by it brings me peace. And, while most of my home is decorated the way I want, there are a few design projects that would make it complete, and one day I'll get around to creating my organic garden, or at least de-weeding the one I've got going now. More than a few years old, my home definitely has a lot of personality. Sometimes you've got to jingle this or hammer that to make it all work, everything always seems to come together in the end, and everyone who comes here is comfortable in this energy.

I guess I could look at my life from a half empty perspective, focusing only on those areas that could be improved but, I really don't feel that's the best way to create better solutions for them. So, even when my glass is only half full, I focus on the fact that I always have exactly what I need, and much of what I want as frosting. Don't get me wrong, I've played the game from both sides, having lots of money, and not having much at all, and I've realized that balance is the best way for me to operate in my reality.

what my life says about my beliefs about money :: I have less than some but, more than others, and can get access to most anything I need in life. Don't get me wrong, I have had my issues with money on both sides of the coin, sometimes having too little, and yes, for me and my reality, having too much. Somewhere along my path I decided I wanted to believe that money was neither a struggle to attain, nor something I needed to let drive me. So, I began focusing more of my time and attention on the things that made me happy, and less on actually making money. That said, I do enjoy my money, as having it allows me to live where I want, buy the items I need, and to travel and pursue the things that I believe will enhance my life experience. And, when life feels overwhelming, or I begin trying to force my dreams into becoming a reality too quickly, I will feel little pinches of financial need. However, and all in all, I walk a line of balance, knowing that I am worthy of love, respect, and yes, money. I constantly remind myself that contributing my talents and values to others is only part of being in the financial flow, as I also allow compensation for my work to easily flow back to me, proportionate to my beliefs.

glass slipper insight :: Now that you've peaked into the minds of how some other princesses' live life, and how they experience money in their reality, I want to help you get even more clarity about yours. To do this, I invite you to write out your answers to the following questions, and see what you really believe about money:

1. What does my financial fairy tale currently look like?
2. Based on my life right now, what are some beliefs that I have about money?

I realize that there are as many ways of believing about money as there are people, so, if you don't resonate with any of the above gals, that's perfectly fine. The reason I presented these princesses in particular was to give you a bird's eye view into a mind that struggles to have money, believing only in lack and limitation, one that demonstrates large sums of money through hard work and effort, and essentially has made it her "king," and the last, being a mind that sees money as a means to an end, nothing more, and nothing less. When you can see and understand, without criticisms or judgment, how a particular belief system creates a very specific reality, then you will be able to better see how your perception of money and relationship to it influences how you experience in your world.

what is money... really

Well, according to several definitions I found online and one I saw in an old dictionary, the basic definition of money is this: money is any object or record

> **darling, in order to create the life you've always dreamed of, you must first know you're worth it.**

that is generally accepted as payment for goods and services, and the repayment of debts in a given socio-economic context or country. Wow! I don't know about you but, that doesn't sound as big or scary as the grownups around me seemed to make money out to be. From the time I can remember understanding the money conversations going on around me, until I was old enough to develop my own ideas, I basically believed that money was this highly coveted thing that you had to work really hard for, sometimes taking multiple jobs that include late night hours away from your family. Then, with whatever money you did make, you needed to be really careful with it or you wouldn't have enough to survive, and that only some people get lucky enough to have lots of it at any high level capacity.

Because far more of us buy into the values we experience about a particular thing over any definition we may read, especially when it comes to something as emotionally charged as money, we need to be careful how we address our current programming, as longtime triggers will no doubt come out to defend themselves against any new ideas. Therefore, in wanting to help you take baby steps that you can build a foundation on, I want to share with you one of the first ideas I remember having that helped me to reshape my own internal programming around money.

Just for a moment, I want to ask you to suspend your personal beliefs about money and consider this instead: money is nothing more than an idea or concept of value that we have agreed upon together as a society. Accordingly, money in and of itself holds no value other than as a means of exchange for us to obtain the things we want and need. Hence, unto itself, money has no power over you and your ability to be happy.

"So Morgan, what you're trying to tell me is that money doesn't influence my ability to be happy?"

Yes! That is what I'm telling you. However, before you go and get all frustrated with me, let me say that your current beliefs about what money is or your attachment to the things that it can buy you, could definitely offer you the experience of feeling happy, in which case, you would see my response as wrong. That said, now that you are starting to be aware that money is only that which you make it out to be, let's go back and take a look at some of the ideas that may have influenced your original programming about money.

why do you believe what you believe about money

I'm not sure that this is true for everyone however, I don't remember being born with any kind of money issues. All of my needs and wants just seem to just show up for me. If I wanted a bottle, toy or blanket, it seemed all I needed to do was make a certain sound, and anyone within earshot in my world would stop what they were doing to give it to me. Unfortunately, as I got older and heard more conversations about lack, limitation, and the powers that be that hold all the money, I began to attach more and more negative and fearful beliefs to it. I remember often thinking that when it was my turn to fend for myself, I might have a really hard time getting any. The interesting part about how we receive our financial programming is that we often don't realize that every experience we witness on the subject influences how we create our personal gospel for what we believe. If never triggered to ponder your relationship with money, you may believe about it only what others have taught you, never questioning those beliefs. However, for those of us who have ever found ourselves in a financial paradigm that didn't fit our picture for happily ever after, we may already be on a path that has us questioning our beliefs. Therefore, I want to draw your attention to some potential programming ideas you may have received about money, so that you can begin shifting any current beliefs that may be blocking you from experiencing it the way that you want to be.

here are some common programming ideas that we receive about money:

phrases :: Do you think that I'm made of money?

Do you think that money grows on trees?

general feeling or meaning :: If these phrases sound like something you heard while growing up, you may be inclined to believe that money is a limited resource that is hard to attain. However, what the person who was saying these things to you really meant was probably something more like "I am doing everything I know how to make money, and the fact that you're asking me to create even more out of the little that I have makes me feel like a failure somehow." However, rather than admit that it was their beliefs about their ability to make money that has them upset, it's far easier for them to blame their lack of it on being because it is a limited resource. This way, they can let themselves off the hook, and not have to take too much responsibility for their lack of making money.

reality :: There is an unlimited supply of money. Just look around you, it comes in paper and metal, and you can find it in banks, grocery stores and even available on the little plastic cards you keep in your wallet. The possibilities for experience money are endless. Therefore, the only limits you experience in producing money in your world are the ones that you believe in.

phrases :: We don't have money because we have the wrong last name.
I wasn't born with a silver spoon in my mouth, ya know!

general feeling or meaning :: When people use phrases like these, hinting that if somehow you were born into a different kind of family, then money would be abundant, comes from a mind that has been taught to give its power away. When they say things like this, the kind of ideas they're usually hiding behind look something like "I don't know what to believe or think to make more money. The only people who seem to have any were born into families that already have lots of it." By rationalizing their lack of money with ideas that only some people can have it, for whatever reason, they are able to release taking any responsibility for being able to create their own financial stability. Accordingly, if they don't believe that it's possible for them to make money because of the family they were born into, then they will never allow their mind to imagine the possibility of experiencing wealth or tapping into the ideas that would allow them to create it.

reality :: The fact is, being born into a wealthy family may give you more access to money at an early age, and therefore might help you develop a wealth consciousness early on. However, even those who are 'born with a silver spoon in their mouth' can experience money troubles, especially if they never develop a prosperity mindset independent of the people who financially support them. Therefore, no matter what financial situation you start from, you must know that you are the one who creates your relationship with money, and your ability to make it, according to your belief. If you want to experience your desired level of financial freedom, you must consciously think the thoughts, and take the necessary action to create that reality.

phrases :: We're poor but, we're happy.
Only ruthless crooks have money.

general feeling or meaning :: The interesting thing about this particular programming about money is that one can often justify their beliefs of not having it by describing themselves as being a 'good person', insinuating somehow that to have money is bad. However, what the person who uses phrases like this usually means is "I haven't figured out how to make the type of money I desire doing what I love. I also fear that I'm not good enough or don't have what it takes to make big money, so to me, anyone who can operate in the financial world like that and succeed must be greedy." These types of thoughts can help the person who doesn't know what to believe to create more money rationalize that they get all their happiness from being able to do what they love for a living. Which is fine however, the law of reciprocity dictates that a positive action must be met with a positive act, therefore, if you are sharing your passions with others, you need to be in a place where you can receive their reciprocity.

reality :: The having of, or not having of money doesn't define you as being good or evil. The only thing having money does is define you as someone who has money in that moment. The opposite is equally true, as the only thing that not having money means is that you don't define or believe yourself to be someone who possess money in that moment. Money in and of itself has no special powers, or good or evil connotation to it, as it is only a means of exchange.

However, if you believe that money is limited, and that there is some kind of magic pill that everyone has taken, but that you don't have access to, then you're going to hold certain resentments towards others that have seemed to figure out how to make it.

phrases :: You ain't nothing in this world without money.

You see, in life there are two types of people, the haves and the have nots, and you want to be one of the haves.

general feeling or meaning :: The person who believes in this type of programming identifies themselves with the materialism of life, feeling that by having more, it makes them better, or at least okay. Because they believe this, they also often believe that anyone who doesn't achieve a certain level of financial success is worthless or has very little value outside of what they can do for them. When someone uses phrases like these, what they usually mean is "I've seen a thing or two in life, and those who've got money have power, and those who don't, don't! I'm a winner in this life, and so is anyone I let be associated with me." Therefore, anyone who doesn't measure up to their financial standards is seen as beneath them, because they fear the lack of having money.

reality :: The reality is money is just money, no matter what else you may want to believe. It's just a means of exchange, and not something that defines you as a person. Yes, a healthy minded person usually experiences money and the things they need to buy with it with general ease however, just because you have money doesn't mean you have a healthy relationship with it. If the having of money is your predominate thought, if it interferes with your ability to genuinely value yourself and others, then it rules your world and you are not being free. When your money defines you, it keeps you in a perpetual state of wanting, and often doing almost anything to get and keep your money.

glass slipper insight :: Can you see where the repetition of ideas like these might have influenced your beliefs about money? Great! Because the good news about making these kinds of discoveries about what you believe, is that when you find ideas that are no longer serving you, you can let them go or reframe them into beliefs that help you better experience your happily ever after.

Did any of those phrases sound familiar to you? In reading them, were you able to see where some of your current beliefs about money may be affecting your ability to experience it how you want to be? Many of us throughout our lives have been programmed to believe that money would make us happy, feel loved and accepted, and depending on our social circle, actually defined our worth as a human being. Wow! That's an awful lot of stuff to put on some little idea we made up to make exchanges for our goods and services convenient and easy.

So, now that we have some idea of where your current programming about money came from, how do we begin to shift you into a financial mindset that is more aligned with your desired fairy tale.

changing the way you think about money

As I've mentioned before, life is like a mirror, constantly reflecting our beliefs back to us by way of our physical experience. When we shift our being and beliefs, so too does our reflection or experience. Therefore, when we desire to bring transformation into our world, we must first start with who we are being, as shifting our beliefs will inevitably create new results in our physical reality. So, now that you are getting a clearer picture about how your beliefs about money effects your ability to produce it, let's explore some ways to shift your perspective about it to one that is congruent with your grandest vision for your castle, kingdom and happily ever after.

eliminating the poverty mindset

So, what do you do when you discover that you've been living with a poverty mindset for all these years? Well, before I offer you some suggestions on what you can do, let me first tell you what you shouldn't do. You shouldn't beat yourself up or feel guilty for any of the times you struggled through a financial situation. The reason being is this: staring at your past and wishing you could change it only keeps you stuck there. To move forward, in a new and more positive way, you have to remind yourself that you created each of those financial experiences for the purpose of leading you to this moment. Yes! Each part of your life process has laid the foundation for you to be able to receive the information you are about to receive. In fact, one of the reasons you were drawn to reading this book is because you are now ready to experience an opportunity to further expand your awareness and relationship with money.

Just to be clear, the reason you have believed in a poverty mentality up until now is because out of all of the experiences you witnessed about money over the course of your life, you chose to give more energy to the ones that reflected lack and limitation, rather than focusing your attention on the experiences where people created money almost effortlessly.

"But Morgan, I never saw any examples of wealth around me when first learning about money!"

I understand that you may believe that to be true but sorry, no excuses allowed here! If you want to expand your consciousness to one that includes making lots of money, then you will have to take responsibility for all the thoughts you think and everything you see. Here, I'll show you what I mean. I'm sure at some point in your life, you drove by a neighborhood, saw a television show or movie, or maybe read in a magazine about people who had lots of money. If so, then you were exposed to wealth. Don't get me wrong, I understand if you tell me that you were exposed to more lack than wealth, or that when you were exposed to money, the people around you made up stories to discourage you from believing you would ever have any. However, we're not looking to further expand the parts of you that resonate with a poverty mindset, so when you look back on your past, it would better serve you if you focused on all the wealth that you have seen.

So, whatever your exposure to wealth thus far, I'm going to assume from here forward that you have seen what being financially wealthy can look like, right? Great! Therefore, without debate, you know that abundance and wealth are possible, correct? Fabulous! If it is possible then for a person to live abundantly, and you are a person, then it is possible for you to be wealthy, right? Yay! You're Getting It! So, what then do you need to know or believe in order to experience life as wealthier? Ah yes, that is the key to wealth, isn't it?

In order to release a poverty mentality from your consciousness, we need to give your mind something new to believe. However, before we start offering your mind all sorts of new programming, I want to give you a fair warning: the ideas and beliefs you hold to be true right now about money have taken your entire lifetime to form, therefore, shifting them immediately into an entirely new belief system might not be a reasonable request to ask.

Accordingly, no matter how gun-ho you feel about taking in all these new ideas right now, I would advise you not to try and force a dramatic shift overnight, which would take an exorbitant amount of focus, will, and energy. If you feel an impulse to plunge in anyway, let me take this moment to remind you that these feelings are coming from the ego, and if you try to force something before you're ready, you will only be able to sustain the belief energy in your idea or imagination for so long before you want to quit. Going about the process like this will make each attempt to believe in your dreams that much harder. Rather, I suggest that you choose to focus on those improved ideas about money that you can nurture most easily, as your success with these will help provide a stronger foundation from which you can create even better ideas to believe.

keys to evicting a poverty mindset

In order to help you further create the belief system of a financially abundant Princess Charming and release any part of you that is resonating with a poverty mentality, I've broken down how certain aspects of a limited belief system influences your being. I did it this way with the hope that if you were able to better understand them, then you would be inspired towards creating a more positive outlook on your ability to demonstrate money.

environment :: As I'm sure you can see by reviewing what may have been some of your original programming about money, environment and the experiences that you subject yourself to play a huge role in influencing your relationship with money. It's been proven that you become like the five people you spend the most time around -- so if money is a part of what you want to see in your reality, -- then you must choose who you spend your time with wisely. I'm not telling you to dump all your friends however, if none of them are experiencing money how you want to be, then how do you expect to raise your consciousness to the level of someone who easily makes large sums of money?

You may be thinking one of two things right now, one being "Morgan, I don't hang out with people just because of what I can gain from them." To which in large part, I would disagree, and here's why: every choice we make, including what friends we hang out with, is to enhance our life experience. Even if you don't choose your friends because of their financial worth, there is no doubt that you do choose them for whatever ways they add value to your life. And, if making money was the main focus of your thought stream, then having friends who equally valued prosperity would also be part of your social scene. The other thought may be something like "If I knew who to hang out with, don't you think I'd be doing it already." To which I have another remedy, I call it "Elevating Your Environment".

elevating your environment :: If the people around you aren't producing much money, no judgment but, then they too are resonating with a poverty mindset. This probably means that many of your conversations about money with them are related to not having any. Therefore, in order to have expanded ideas and conversations about money, you need to place yourself in situations with people who demonstrate it more easily. If right now, you don't know anyone who is doing well with money, then I invite you to read several biographies or yes, watch some on T.V. about inspiring individuals' self-made success stories. Fill your mind with as many ideas about wealth as you can so that you are inspired to take action towards creating it in your life. This action may look like going back to school, attending professional networking meetings, or even going to trade show expos to meet other people having success in a field that interest you. Whatever the method, the only way to experience a prosperous environment is to create it first in your mind, and then follow through by taking action when inspiration hits you.

language :: Equally important to your ability to create money is the language you use to describe it. If you are constantly using language that reinforces that you don't have enough and that you may never get ahead, then you are perpetuating the ideas of lack and limitation in your mind. You can't walk around saying things like "I can't afford this." and "I'll never have enough to be able to do that." and think that somehow the money you need is going to appear in your lap magically. It just doesn't work that way. When you give the power of your voice to your limited thinking about money, you are further setting into motion the reflection of that belief in your physical reality.

"If that's true, then what do I say when I really don't have enough money to do the things I want to do then?"

Glad you asked, because this is a part of the process that most people get tripped up on when they begin shifting their programming around money. If you want to experience more money in your life, you have to do what I call "Lifting Your Language", to a vocabulary that is congruent with having the abundance you desire.

lifting your language :: When you don't have enough money to do the things that you desire, instead of saying something like "I don't have enough." replace it with a phrase such as "I'm choosing to spend my money in other places right now." Even if all you have is five dollars to your name, when you shift your language to one that affirms that you have a choice in how you want to spend the money you have, then you are reaffirming in your mind that you do indeed have money to spend. Crazy, right? The very act of affirming and reaffirming to yourself that you have money, triggers the very ideas necessary to your thought stream to create more of it in your reality.

habits :: Any single action that you take can eventually lead to a habit. Therefore, all of your current producing, spending and saving habits, good or bad, first started out as a single idea that you pursued. For instance, while paying one bill last minute might not have affected your entire financial scene, if that one act turned into a habit of regular late pays, then you would quickly find yourself in a state of financial misery. Accordingly, if you are tired of experiencing money in the limited ways that you currently are, then you need to start creating new habits for relating to money in a way that you want to be. To do this, you begin by first shifting your money mentality. For example, if you're the kind of person who doesn't save their money, or has never donated a portion of their earnings to an organization that inspires them, then now may be the time to consider doing both.

"Um, Morgan, I don't think you get it. I don't make enough money to save, and I sure as heck don't have enough to give it away."

Well, before I get into how to shift that idea, I want to direct you back to the section on "Lifting Your Language", as perhaps you weren't paying attention when I explained about what happens when you give a voice to your money fears. Yes, watching your language applies all the time! Now, if you are ready to shift your habits to ones that may better support you, I'd like to introduce you to the idea of "Helping Your Habits".

helping your habits :: If you're thinking " 'Help my Habits', what in the heck does that mean?", I'm glad, because that gives me a chance to explain the power of healthy habit forming. When we form a habit, good or bad, it means our subconscious mind has accepted a certain set of actions as a way to deliver a desired experience to us. These habits, even if the original act was only a temporary fix, can tint our perspective and the ways in which we engage with life. Therefore, if you are experiencing less money than you want to be, then you are engaged in a habitual thought system that continues to feed you ideas that you can't experience as much money as you want to be.

The reason we have habits is because they provide us with payoffs. The payoff I find most often associated with people lacking money is not taking full responsibility for what they make, because they're always able to rationalize their lack with there not being enough. However, just as habits can work against you in your desire to have more money, when created more mindfully, they can actually support you. For example, as I mentioned in our session on food together, something as simple as choosing whole foods on a regular basis can turn into a habit that provides you with the results of vibrant health and developing the habit of brushing your teeth daily leads to a life with fewer cavities. Habits are very powerful things and should be treated accordingly.

To make it easier for you to create better habits in your relationship with money, I wrote out a list of 'real world' actions you can take to start you on your journey. While no single one of them alone will shift your entire being, the point of incorporating a series of small doable habits such as these will help you to reduce your poverty mindset until you can replace it with a wealth mentality.

real world actions to help eliminate a poverty mindset

Affirm all of the good things you currently have in your life

Take time every day to be grateful for all that you have

Find a way to donate your time to those less fortunate than you

Read biographies about people going
beyond their circumstances

Donate a portion of your income to
organizations that inspire you

Act generously as often as it feels
comfortable and you are able.

Take an inventory of all your talents,
and the ways that you can use them to help others.

Be mindful of how you spend your money,
knowing each purchase defines you.

it's only money... and not your king

Okay, so unlike your poverty mentality princess counterpart, you are demonstrating money to the tune of a small fortune, and you're rather pleased with yourself but, how's your life outside of your pursuits of money? I know, you've got friends, family and get to travel, as well as see and have the latest of everything but, how far away ever are worries about money? Not budging, huh? Okay, I thought getting through to you might be tough, as I know your self- esteem is based on your money. However, before I bring out the big guns as to what really drives you towards success, what if I just mentioned that one of the only reasons you cling onto the ideas of money that you do is because, like your friends who struggle with ideas of lack, you also believe that money is a limited resource, and more specifically, worry about who you would be without it.

Are you with me yet?

Okay, good. Just because you are demonstrating large sums of money in your life, doesn't mean you are experiencing true wealth and abundance. If you are a slave to money, and the material goods you buy with it define your being, then your ego is winning the "I'm so special, look at me for being rich." game, at the expense of all the other amazing things you could be experiencing. Yes, your ego, that beautiful part of you that drives you towards success when used correctly, can flip on you in a moment of fear, and influence you to sell your soul to possess whatever it is that will make you feel special again, including money.

So, what is the litmus test for knowing whether or not you're living a life of balanced abundance or if you are a slave to your money? Well, everyone is a different however, here are some questions you can ask yourself to help you further clarify how and why you demonstrate money in the ways that you do.

1. Do you buy something because it brings you joy, or because you believe that possessing it will validate you or increase your credibility?
2. Do you put pursuing success in front of your health, quality time with your family, or other hobbies you'd like to pursue if you weren't busy spending all your time earning and managing your money?
3. Even after you land the 'big deal', or sign a lucrative contract, are you still concerned with 'what's next' and how you're going to earn even more money?
4. Do you let your perception of another person's wealth be a determiner as to whether or not you would pursue an association with them, romantically or otherwise?

If who you are being right now resonates with a positive response to these questions, I would say you may want to re-evaluate your relationship with money. Don't get nervous, I'm not telling you to give up anything, I just want to invite you to take a different look at how you can use money, and still have your happily ever after.

"Okay Morgan, I get that I don't need to be all about the money but really, if I've got all the cash and material possessions I could ever want or need, then how is my relationship with money keeping me from fully being princess charming?"

If you are always worried about how much money you, or the people around you have, then your beliefs about money are clouding your perspective and ability to live free. Just because you are in possession of money and nice things, doesn't mean you've created a wealth consciousness internally. If you go after money to look good doing something, or to impress others, then you are not living a life of authenticity. True wealth comes from being healthy and happy, and spending your time doing the things that you want to do. However, if your primary focus is making money, rather than being able to experience the full-spectrum of joy that life has to offer you, you will only see the bottom-line, which may be good for your stockholders but, not so good for your quality of life.

In case you haven't heard the many reports in news, television and other online media, it's be proven that stress is one of the biggest causes of a whole slew of the diseases we now produce in our bodies. When you obsess about money, your stress levels can't help but increase, which in turn makes you more vulnerable to anxiety, weight gain, and catching any number of unhealthy things. Additionally, you rob yourself of the simple joys in life such as watching children play, experiencing nature's beauty, and engaging in intimate relationships that are not based on money.

"Hmmmm, I suppose that I can admit that I may be a little bit of a slave to my money, but, what do I do to change it without losing everything I've earned?"

treating money as the tool it's supposed to be

First off, let me say that in no way do I want you to lose anything, as that would not be the life of Princess Charming. What I am inviting you to do however, is take a simple inventory of the all the significant things in your life and decide whether or not they're worth the price you're really paying for them. If in fact you go through this little inventory exercise, I'm quite sure that you will discover organic ways you could downsize your life, while living a more fulfilling and sustainable life-style. Just so we're clear, I'm not talking about cutting back your expenses and trying to live at the same capacity, only with less money. I'm talking about re-prioritizing your values, so that you are spending less time focusing on money, and more time on the many other things that can make you happy.

> **"Too many people spend money they haven't earned, to buy things they don't want, to impress people they don't like."**
> **~ Will Smith, Actor**

For those of you whose ego is going into total meltdown as you begin to ponder a smaller life, let me help you soothe yourself. Downsizing does not mean failure, or that you're less than in anyway, as it actually takes more courage to choose a life that is authentically congruent with all your beliefs and desires, than to maintain appearances so that you can impress others that you may or may not care about. Releasing your need to strive for money so that you can receive approval from others allows you to make room for new ideas to come through. When you discover who you really are and what you want, you may find out that there's a whole lot out there that you love that doesn't require any money.

So, now that you're actually contemplating a slight downshift, you know, for your health and all, how do you go about doing it in such a way that doesn't cause even more stress in your world? To simplify it in a way I felt would be the least scary to you, I created a list of 'real world' actions and ideas for you to consider as a you create a more sustainable life for yourself. Again, while no one act is a cure all to healing any of the false ideas you hold about money, by practicing new ways of being with it, you will expand your awareness, which will then put you in a better position to create it in a way that's more comfortable to you.

real world actions to downshift into a more sustainable lifestyle

Create more free time for yourself by saying "No." to things that you really don't have to do, t o discover your real passions and hobbies.

Be more conscious of your consumption habits. Are there times that convenience is getting the better of your bank account?

Limit the number of services you purchase to those things that you don't have time for, or can't do more cost effectively yourself.

Don't buy designer everything when other products will do just as nicely.

One last reminder as it relates to creating a life that's uniquely you: living a life of financial balance or sustainability is NOT about self-denial, as you shouldn't give up the things that matter to you. Just take inventory of those things that aren't really necessary to your happily ever after.

different strokes for different, umm princesses

At the end of the day, regardless of what you may believe, not everyone wants to experience life, or money, in the same way. Amazing, I know. Some of us want to live the life of luxury, experiencing every creature comfort imaginable, while others of us want to just kick back and enjoy the simple life. Therefore, to help you further define who you want to be with money, I've created some 'Magical Manifesting Insights', that will help lead you to a thought stream that supports your financial dreams. In order to get the best out of these insights, I highly recommend reading each question in your desired category and writing down the answers. In doing so, you will have already taken your idea from the unseen, a random thought in your head, to a physical manifestation that you can see as organized words written on paper. This demonstration is the beginning of your ability to see that you can create the abundance you want to experience as Princess Charming.

MAGIC MANIFESTING INSIGHT :: Want to Create a Life of Luxury?

If you want to live a life of money and luxury, then you must be a "YES!" to everything associated with money and luxury that you see. Never doubt that all your financial needs will be met abundantly. For every time you resonate positively with a particular idea, you send a signal out into the Universe that you want to experience more of that in your life. Therefore, whether it's a dime you find on the street, or a new job opportunity, you have to look for and praise every opportunity you see in your life to experience money the way you want to be.

QUESTIONS ::

1. What are some things I can do right now to experience more luxury in my world?
2. What are some talents I can perform to demonstrate my worth back to me?
3. Where can I show more gratitude for the ways I'm already living the 'high life'?

MAGIC MANIFESTING INSIGHT :: Want to Create a life of Simplicity?

If what you want is a life of simplicity, then you must focus on those things that are already running smoothly in your world. If you want more calm and serene energy in and around you, as hard as it may be at first, you must look away from those things that trigger feelings of stress, get you angry, or otherwise knock you off your balance. This is not to say you should stick your head in the sand but, more specifically, if you have things in your life that put you on edge, it's time to look at new and more peaceful ways of making your way in life.

QUESTIONS ::

- What are some things I can do right now to experience more simplicity in my world?
- How can I clarify my passions and work in a way that allows me to be most productive?
- Where can I show more gratitude for the simplicity that already exists in my life?

MAGIC MANIFESTING INSIGHT :: Want to Create a Life of Material Comforts & Ease?

Ah... so, you want a little bit of each, some of life's luxuries blended in with the right amount simplicity, well then you must create a line of balance that reflects your values in each. A little confused? That's okay, creating a balanced life often can be. What you need to do to create this life is define for yourself those things that you want to experience in luxury, and those areas where you rather have simplicity. For instance, you may decide that high-end restaurants, all organic food, and five star wines are all you're going to consume but, as it relates to buying purses or shoes, a medium quality with a little style will do.

In creating a life of material comforts and ease, you may decide that spending more time with your family is of more value than saying "Yes!" to traveling out of town for one more business meeting, or if there's a financial goal on the line, then you may put in a few extra hours for the time off later. Just as it is with any type of life you're trying to create, being more aware and conscious of the things you give focus to will allow you to better create your fairy tale.

Last thought :: By focusing on the things you want to do, you actually create more time in your life to do them, including making money more simply.

QUESTIONS ::

1. What I can do right now to experience more balance in my world?
2. What are some ways I can combine my love of simple things and modern luxury?
3. Where can I show more gratitude for the balance that already exists in my life?

gratitude

You didn't think we would go through an entire session about money together and leave out how much gratitude plays a part in your experience of it, did you? Because everything we give our focus to grows, gratitude is a feeling we want to give as much energy to as we are able. For it is by demonstrating gratitude for your possessions, life experiences, and your very being, that you create within yourself a belief system wherein there is much to be grateful for. When you vibrate at a level of gratitude, you are sending out a signal to the Universe that what you want reflected back to you are experiences to be grateful for.

Need more reasons to believe that gratitude is key to your (financial) well-being? In several studies on gratitude from national and international research institutions to personal ones I've conducted with my own clients, it has been proven time and again that gratitude has positive effects on our physical, mental and emotional well-being, as well as adding to our relationships with others.

The reason for this is that you cannot experience gratitude, and lack, jealously, limitation or fear in the same moment. Don't believe me? Go ahead, try it. Right now, take a moment to focus on being grateful for something in your life, and once you're fully in that space, see if there are any lower energetic emotions coming through…magic, right?

Yes, I like to think of gratitude as a magic little pill, whenever I'm feeling low and need to feel balanced again, I know by repeating the things I'm grateful for in my head, I will always shift my energy. If by chance, you find yourself in a state where anger, fear or sadness has taken hold, and you're not ready to get into a space of gratitude just yet, I highly recommend deep breathing or going for a walk until you can calm down, also try turning on some soothing music until you can get to a place where you can let ideas of gratitude permeate your mind again.

A huge benefit to having gratitude be a central part of your belief system is that it leaves no room for other toxic emotions such as jealousy, envy and resentment to penetrate your thought stream, and hence, keeps you from sliding into a victim or poverty mentality. When you create a habit of being grateful, your mind will constantly look for those things in your life to be grateful for, including the abundance that you are already experiencing.

Perhaps you could think about it this way: if you've ever experienced a time when you were getting ready to buy a new car, and you suddenly started noticing 'your model' all over the road, then you've witnessed the result of your mind trying to deliver a desired experience to you. Therefore, if you tell your mind to focus on abundance and gratitude, your mind will seek out as many reasons as possible to experience abundance and gratitude, and will soon no longer be able to resonate with ideas in limitation and lack, because they are no longer concepts that you give your energy to.

create more gratitude in your life

I'm sure by this point, you've heard all sorts of ideas on how to focus on gratitude. Many motivational speakers and talk show hosts talk about gratitude journals, and some movies and spiritual gurus have even shared the idea of gratitude rocks and while I'm sure all of these methods help people focus more on gratitude, my favorite gratitude exercise is something that I call the "10/10". However, before I share it with you, I must confess that different versions of this exercise came across my path before I created my own unique version of it. Yes, as it is with many great ideas, of which this is surely one, we all blend and revise ideas, theories and visions that we're exposed to so that we can create our own unique reality. Speaking of which, can't wait to see how you're going to blend, borrow and revise all the ideas you're learning here.

That said, I have never given the '10/10' exercise to a single friend or client who, when they followed it, didn't feel noticeably better about themselves within a week, and subsequently, experienced quantifiable results within 30 to 45 days. I'm not saying that they achieved rock star status in that time, though a few have. However, my reason for sharing this with you is because everyone I've encountered who has done this exercise ended up living clearer, and experiencing more positive movement towards creating a life of their own design, in almost no time, and that's a fairy tale we all can believe in.

glass slipper insight | The "10/10" Exercise ::

Each day, at around the same time so as to develop a ritual, you will write out ten things you are grateful for. These things may stay the same from day to day or they may change regularly, and most likely you will have combinations thereof. The point is to keep the list fresh, so that you are spending this time aligning your energy with GRATITUDE.

Example :: I am grateful for my home and family.

Next, write a list of the ten things you are in the process of manifesting. Again, many of the things on your list will remain the same, and many of them will vary from day to day, and here's why:

If you write out a bunch of desires that you believe are 'hard' to experience, such as, "I want 5 million dollars right now," it sends your current thought stream into chaos, for it has no idea how to go from creating your currently reality to creating the one that you now desire. Therefore, if you ask yourself to make these huge leaps, rather than allowing a belief system to develop that will support your new idea, to protect itself, your mind will feed you a steady stream of fearful ideas to talk you out of it.

However, if you create a blended list, one that includes ideas that your mind perceives as 'easy', such as "Girls Night Out!" with things you feel you need to expand towards to receive, you will get a better result. This occurs because, when you accomplish the 'easy' things on your list, you are actually creating the foundation you need to believe in even bigger ideas for your life.

freedom and responsibility

More than their desire for more money, the trend I've noticed in most people is that they actually want to experience more freedom. Freedom to buy the things they want and to spend their time where and how they choose. In these observations, I've also noticed that most people don't have a particularly hard time generating the desire for more money, however, taking responsibility for doing what is necessary to experience it, well, that can sometimes be a different story.

If you want to create anything in your life, including more money, you must first utilize the ideas and resources currently available to you, as your ability to use them effectively demonstrates that you are responsible enough to handle even more. This probably isn't a new concept for you, as it was programmed into most of us pretty organically by parents who often only doled out new privileges if we were willing to take on more responsibility. For example, if you wanted to go out and party with your friends, I'm sure you had to prove you wouldn't get in trouble or miss curfew. The key to making this concept work for you is by identifying where and how you need to take on more responsibility now, so that you can experience more money.

In order to have more free time, you must first create the ideas in your mind of a life that affords that time to you. You begin to create this time by taking more responsibility for how you currently spend what you have, maneuvering different activities around until you create your days exactly how you want them to be. The same is true with your finances, you must first demonstrate total responsibility for your financial obligations, including the commitment to saving some for yourself, every time you get paid. When you are responsible enough to pay all of your obligations up front, you will experience the freedom and confidence to spend whatever is left over however you choose.

In addition to taking responsibility for what you have, you must also take responsibility for the things that you desire. This means not buying into the limited thinking about a failing economy or that your job is the only way you can make money. Rather, I'd invite you to entertain all sorts of random ideas about ways that you would like to make money. Not that every one of them is for you however, when you begin to focus your intention on the fact that there are other financial opportunities out there, your mind will search out those opportunities to reflect your beliefs back to you through your reality. If focused on long enough, with positive intention and energy, these considerations will eventually lead you to your perfect opportunity to make money like your desired Princess Charming.

glass slipper insight :: Now if you want more freedom, then it's time to take responsibility... how are you going to create your fairy tale with money from here forward?

Write your new financial fairy tale, the kind that evolves steadily and that you can believe in. Imagine your world full of all the freedom you've ever desired, and all you need to do is continue to focus on it. The story is now up to you...what do you want to believe about money?

_____
_____
_____
_____
_____
_____
_____
_____
_____
_____
_____
_____
_____
_____
_____

one last thing before we move onto the mediterranean of meaning...

If you spend your life chasing money, it will always elude you, for the very act of wanting it, pushes the experience of it further away from you. If however, you can focus on living your life on authentic purpose, energetically pursuing your passions, you will find all the financial resources you can believe to support you in living the way that you choose. ~ 🖤 M

SESSION SIX

meaning

happiness

you come to me, unexpectedly

then vanish, in an instant

I search for you, hoping for a new point of view

only to discover you, when I least expect to

you are part of me, yet seem so hard to feel

often making me wonder, is happiness even real

meaning

Everything you want, you want because you believe it will make you feel HAPPY! ~♥M

I'm guessing that when you saw the title "Meaning," you just knew that I was going to go into some deep and heavy spiritual space, elaborating on your place in the cosmos, who you are in relationship to God, and the destiny of your life. Well, you're kind of right, but not quite, as we're actually going to discuss being happy. I will, of course, be using spiritual insights throughout our time together however, I really want to focus your attention on happiness, because most of the people I see who want to experience more meaning are usually doing so in order to increase their quality of living. And given the fact that you're reading a book about creating your own happily ever after, I would imagine that this might potentially be you too.

Before we dive head first into the pool of happiness, I want to take a moment to share with you the basic premise as to how I understand the meaning of life. I have come to believe that the meaning or purpose of life is that which you declare it to be. Sound a little confusing? That's okay. I thought so too the first time I heard the concept. Perhaps thinking of it this way will help. When someone declares that they have discovered their purpose, what they really mean is, "I have had enough positive reactions or experiences, while entertaining this idea about me, that I now know through my ability to produce these happy feelings, that this must be the path for me." This is why the desire for us to know our purpose - or to give meaning to our life is so strong; because we inherently know that when we are living our purpose - or doing the thing that gives our life meaning, we experience happiness.

This is why I will be using happiness, and the ways it influences your ability to define meaning for you and your life, as the basis of our "Meaning" session together. Let me pre-warn you, if you have never thought of happiness in the ways that you are going to read about here, you might dismiss some of the ideas as too simplistic. However, I assure you of their value, as I have firsthand knowledge of their positive impact on my life, and on the lives of my clients and friends, who have applied the insights I'm about to share with you. I know you want to create a happily ever after of your own design - accordingly, we are going to cover several aspects of how your thought stream, beliefs, emotions, and feelings all influence your ability to produce that reality.

our internal compass

I'm sure by now you've come to certain conclusions about what happiness is for yourself, however, I'd like to suggest that happiness is our natural state of being - or as I sometimes call it - our "baseline" emotion. I refer to it as our baseline emotion because unless some internal story or outside stimuli evokes a fear-based idea into our thought stream, our natural state of being is happiness or bliss. The reason we experience this happiness is because when we're not being distracted by undesirable thoughts and ideas, we allow ourselves to be in total alignment with whatever we call "Source Energy", which in turn produces feelings of happiness. When we feel happy, it means that our thoughts, ideas, choices, and actions are all in alignment with who we say we want to be.

glass slipper insight :: There are two basic ways of understanding how to produce feelings of "happiness" for yourself. In order for you to see them more clearly, I've broken them down into formulas. One is based on a more linear system of thinking, the other, a whole new way to create the life of Princess Charming.

When reading each idea, ask yourself which formula you believe would get, and keep you more motivated to achieve your dreams.

linear formula for happiness :

FOCUSED THOUGHTS + DELIBERATE ACTION =
WHO WE WANT TO BE (DESIRED RESULTS) = BE HAPPY

becoming princess charming formula for happiness :

CHOOSING TO BE HAPPY = HAPPY THOUGHTS = HAPPY
ACTIONS = CREATING MORE OPPORTUNITIES TO EXPERIENCE
BEING HAPPY

"So, if being happy is the ultimate bliss, why then do we even have all those other emotions?"

Well, simply put, all of our emotions serve us equally in their ability to help guide us towards the things we want to be and experience in life. It's funny because when I have conversations with people about how to live more fulfilling lives, a question such as "Why can't we all be born with a GPS system for our lives — something that leads us to the things that will make us happy?" often comes up, to which I respond, "You do!" Each of us is born with an internal compass, helping us to navigate the choices in our lives, it's called, our emotions. Like a compass or GPS system, our emotions provide us with up-to-the-moment navigational advice through our feelings.

Our feelings serve as internal signals letting us know whether or not the thoughts we are thinking are on track to manifesting a desired experience. If you feel off-balanced, stressed, scared, embarrassed, anxious, or let's face it, anything other than happiness, that's your own internal mechanism letting you know that your thoughts are NOT on track with your desired fairy tale. Accordingly, when we feel happy or are in a state of joy, contentment, or bliss, these are signals letting us know that the thoughts we are thinking are leading us to our desired reality.

understanding our emotional compass

While happiness, peace, and joy are usually our desired feelings, because they make us feel good, every emotion we feel is meant to let us know how we are thinking about what we are creating and experiencing in our world. When your thoughts are on track with your desired experiences, then your feedback system will offer you a range of positive feelings and more ideas to help you stay in that positive space. However, when you experience negative feelings, this means that your current thought stream is creating a future experience or responding to the one in front of you as something that you do not want. Therefore, whenever you feel anything less than happy, that's your clue to check your thinking to see where you need to refocus on those ideas that will help you feel happy.

To help you better understand how your emotions work, and what signal it is that they're trying to send you, I've broken down certain aspects surrounding some of the more challenging ones that people experience. While I know there are a variety of emotions that are felt at different levels by different people at various times in their lives, I've chosen the emotional descriptions here to provide you a foundation with which to understand how your negative emotions affect you. By understanding these signals, you will be in a better position to develop the necessary coping skills to get back to a state of happiness, so that you can live your happily ever after however you choose.

emotions that let us know that our thinking is off track

anger

what it is :: Anger is an emotional response to the way we process certain types of fear triggers. These emotions can show up as feelings of defensiveness, frustration, irritation, criticism, judgment, jealously, bitterness, or impatience.

what they're there to tell you :: When you feel anger, your feedback system is signaling to you that whatever you are experiencing, by way of your thoughts, is creating the feeling of wanting to protect or defend yourself. These feelings are also often experienced when we make up negative stories in our head about what other people are going to say or do to us, which can cause us to get angry and put our guard up before we even find ourselves in the actual experience.

restore your good feelings :: When something in your experience causes you to feel angry, before reacting to it from this space, take a moment to calm yourself as best as you can. You can do this most easily by closing your eyes and literally 'stilling' your emotions, until your whole systems feels perfectly calm or as close to calm as you can get within your time frame. When you're ready, process the experience as best as you're able and see who you want to show up as (angry, calm, happy, etc.) in relationship to it. When you choose who you want to be first, you will find that you're less reactive to the words and actions of other people, as you will be more focused on who you are being. This elevated mindset allows you to not take the idiosyncrasies of others personally, which keeps you from getting angry as often and leads to you living a happier life, more consistently.

sadness ::

what it is :: Sadness is also a way that we process experiences that cause us to feel afraid. These emotions can show up as feelings of depression, isolation, loneliness, guilt, unworthiness, self-loathing, or anxiousness.

what they're there to tell you :: When you are feeling sad, your emotional feedback system is signaling to you that your thoughts about what you're creating will fall short of your desired experience in some way. These feelings are also usually associated with giving our power away, telling ourselves that others are responsible for our happiness, and then becoming discouraged when they don't meet our expectations.

restore your good feelings :: By reminding ourselves that the only one responsible for our happiness is us, we can usually release the ideas in our thought stream that tells us that others control our ability to feel happy. When we feel sad, it's usually associated with the experience of loss, whether it's the loss of a loved one, a home, a job or missing out on an opportunity we believed would make us feel happy. However, when we focus on the fact that happiness is a state of mind that we can choose, and that by our very choosing of it, we will attract new experiences in which to feel happy, it makes holding on to the 'yucky stuff', far less appealing.

fear ::

what it is :: Fear is the emotional response to thinking thoughts or experiencing situations that make you believe that you're alone and disconnected from "Source Energy." These feelings of fear often show up as tension, worry, doubt, nervousness, scarcity, and limitation, as well as terror when exposed to things the mind categorizes as horrific.

what they're there to tell you :: The only time you feel any kind of fear is when you believe that you are separate from that which created everything. When you forget, or your thought-stream feeds you ideas that you are anything less than a magnificent being, created with and by Source Energy, then you will experience varying levels of fear. In other words, fear is the emotional response to anything you're creating in your reality that would cause you to feel scared, as these feelings are meant to reflect to you that your thoughts are way off track, and you need to choose a better thought stream quickly.

how to soothe it to restore your good feelings :: The first thing you need to do anytime you feel fear is to remind yourself that you are experiencing the situation in front of you according to your perspective (beliefs). Therefore, any experience that your fear-based thought stream created will dissipate when you replace it with a loving thought stream. Let me repeat, anytime you feel fear, it means your thought stream is feeding you ideas that disconnect your consciousness from feeling source energy and being happy. So, when these feelings show up, take note to see where and how your thoughts are taking you down the wrong path, so you can simply shift them back.

restoring your good feelings

Stop your physical body from
whatever you are doing.

Find a quiet space, even if it's only in your head.

Begin to take deep breaths, matching
the inhale and the exhale.

Close your eyes, and begin to feel
yourself become as still as glass.

Focusing solely on your breath repeat the words:
"I AM Love - I AM Calm - I AM Peace".

Stay in this space until you feel the chaos
spinning in your head has subsided.

how does being happy motivate you towards better choices

As perhaps you are now beginning to see on an even deeper level, our emotions not only have a direct influence on how we perceive life but, they are actually the direct response we have to observing or experiencing our thought stream in a physical reality. When we are in a happy or high state of being, it often feels like we're in a magical flow, able to make clearer choices to create our happy experiences more rapidly. This happens because when we are in a happy state our internal feedback signal is letting us know that our entire being is congruent with the moment we're experiencing. Therefore, happiness is more than "just" our baseline emotion; it's also a huge motivator that ignites our imagination so that we can create bigger and better realities for ourselves.

happiness and our ego

Based on the "Effects-of-Happiness" we've been discussing thus far, it may seem as though I'm saying that happiness, gratitude, and love are the only feelings that motivate us towards pursuing our goals. If that were true, then life would probably be much simpler to navigate, and the process of creating desired experiences would be that much easier, but, it's not. Therefore, in an effort to help you create your happy experiences more responsibly, I want to once again address that very special aspect of ourselves, the ego. As I've mentioned in some of our other sessions together, when understood and used consciously as a life tool, the ego can be one of our greatest allies in the evolution process. Its ability to make us feel separate creates opportunities to help us witness our ideas and beliefs through the eyes of our internal observer. It is from the observer perspective that we can see the contrast between who we are and what we experience, so that we can grow. However, when it comes to defining what will create genuine happiness in your life, you and your ego will often butt heads.

Because your ego has such a heavy influence over your thought stream, including pushing you towards doing things you may not yet be ready for, you must be weary when your internal motivation is pushing you too fervently to jump into an idea with both feet. The reason behind this is that when we first declare ourselves to be a particular idea (i.e. a writer, mother, business person, or healer), we trigger an internal evolutionary process that continues to expand our consciousness in a particular direction, until we reach a level of belief that is equal to us having the experience of being that thing in this physical reality. Though the adrenaline rushes associated with the feelings we get when our ego gets ahold of an idea can be very seductive, if you have not yet developed a consciousness that can hold on to that idea long enough to make it a reality, you will then quickly find yourself experiencing quick sand, and may lose that version of your dream all together.

glass slipper insight :: To assess whether or not an idea for happiness is coming from your authentic being or your ego, put it to a little test. If when you follow the thought stream that originates from this idea, you can see where you would enjoy the process of growing organically, because you have a genuine passion for the experience, chances are your idea for happiness came from an authentic place. However, if when you put your idea up for further scrutiny you discover that you really only want the end result associated with that choice, i.e. the money or prestige, chances are it's an ego-based idea, and you probably want to go back to your imagination until you can allow a more authentic idea to surface.

emotions are our primary manifestation

While happiness is the emotional feedback we receive to let us know that our thoughts are on track with what we want to experience, the very reason we want to experience anything at all is because we want to experience the emotional response we believe it will generate within us. Therefore, your primary motivation towards a certain experience is not about the experience in and of itself but is more specifically about the feelings you believe the experience will provide you by having it. Don't believe me? Okay. I'll give you some examples that may help you better understand my point. When you go to an amusement park, the reason you are motivated to stand in line for hours for your favorite ride is because of the feeling it provides you when you're having the experience. The same is true when you choose a particular genre of movie, if you are feeling or want to feel romance, you pick a romantic film, and if you want to get spooked, you would probably be more inclined to choose a horror film.

You see, we are feeling beings - everything we observe, experience, or think about generates an emotion we can feel. So then, our desire to have a house, car, job, children, or even prince charming is so that we can feel the feelings we believe we will have when we "get it." Don't get me wrong, I'm not insinuating that your desire to own your own business or to be the best "Mrs." in the world aren't real, I'm just saying that once you understand that you are pursuing the experience for the feeling it gives you, then you can learn to generate those feelings first, in order to further catapult you towards the experience.

happiness isn't something you find, but rather a chosen state of mind.

happily ever after is a state of mind

Because of how most of us have been programmed throughout the course of our lives, we have come to believe that it is our physical experiences that influence our state of mind. If this is your belief system, the most probable way this programming took root in your mind was through the repetition of having what you would call a "good experience," which was then followed by the experience of "good feelings." Because this process seemed to duplicate itself over and again in your life, you developed a firm belief that it was your experience that drove your mood, never giving much thought to the fact that it might actually work the other way around. However, when you discover that you can choose your state of mind first, you will experience real magic in your life, as it is from this place of happiness that you can better create a life of your own design.

Curious? Good!

When you choose to feel happy first, you raise your energy level to a place that positively impacts your thought stream and decision-making faculties, which subsequently increases the quality of the life experiences you produce. Accordingly, choosing to create your life from a space of happiness actually increases your ability to produce happy experiences, especially when the alternative is selecting random experiences with the hopes that they will make you happy. In order to capitalize on your power to choose your own happiness, you must begin by making peace with who you are and what you've currently created in your world. That's right! If you want to manifest all the love, abundance, health, passion, and creativity that you currently dream of, you must make peace with the car, the job, the relationships, the home, and the amount of money in your bank account that your beliefs have created thus far. When you make peace with yourself about who you are and the reality you're creating, you allow your emotional feedback system to go into 'neutral', which then allows you to focus on, and generate the feelings of happiness you desire. It is from this accepting, peaceful, and happy state that you are able to close the gap between the parts of you that define yourself as separate or a victim to life's whims, and the infinitely creative being that you know you really are. When this gap is closed, you feel more empowered, more inspired and more like the Princess Charming who is creating her happily ever after, better than ever before.

our real fairy godmother :: happiness

Yes, my fella earth travelers, each of us was born with a very real fairy godmother - the kind who helps grant us our every wish on the path to becoming the Princess Charming we've always dreamed of. Sometimes I call her "Love" or "Gratitude" but, I usually refer to her as "Happiness," for whenever Love, Gratitude, and Happiness show up in our lives, so too, do our dreams and desires.

In order to show you how happiness works like a fairy Godmother to positively impact the quality of your life, I'm going to first demonstrate its influence on your ability to make positive choices on the main areas we've already covered for your life. My goal in doing this is to show you why choosing to put happiness first in all of your decision-making will always increase the quality of your choice.

food ::

In our session on food together, we read about how all the Princesses experienced their relationship with food, exactly according to their belief. If you noticed, no matter what their specific issue - starving, over eating, or eating according to their peer group, each one struggled with internal beliefs about themselves in relationship to food that created the experience of feeling unhappy.

what happiness can do :: When we choose to be happy before we make our food choices, we get to experience our desired result of being happy now, relying less on the food to stimulate that experience within us. Additionally, when we feel happy and tempting food choices come our way, we have the energy and confidence to sit back and observe if making a particular choice is in alignment with our desired results. If not, our higher mood and energy empowers us to more easily turn it away.

real world result :: When your tummy is grumbling on the way home and you know you don't have any food in the fridge, if you're focused on being happy, your thought stream will be filled with multiple food ideas to help you stay happy.

Accordingly, your happy state will help you feel more empowered to make a healthy food choice, picking up a smoothie or something from your local health food store, over choosing a greasy fast food option.

fitness ::

No matter what your level of fitness, if you are coming from an unhappy or low vibrating mood, your workout routine will suffer. If you continue to stay in this unhappy place, then not only will your fitness goals suffer, but, you may give it up all together.

what happiness can do :: Before we even get you to the workout itself, let me tell you how happiness will influence your ability to reach your fitness goals. A large reason many of us workout, in addition to the health benefits and how it makes us look, is for how it makes us feel: happy. When we choose to be happy first, we feel more inspired, our energy increases, and we have all the motivation we need to complete any workout routine.

real world result :: When you wake up in the morning, instead of hitting the "snooze" button on your alarm, your happy feelings will give you the inspiration and energy to pop, or at least crawl out of bed, and head on over to the gym for your workout routine. If over half the battle to achieving success in anything is showing up, you want happy to be an ally in getting you there.

men ::

Did you notice how many of the princesses in our session on Men seemed to be unhappy, often blaming their partner for their misery? Because, if everyone we're in a relationship with serves as a direct reflection of who we're being, there is no way we can expect a Prince Charming to reflect back feelings of happiness to us if we're being Ms. Crabby Pants, now can we?

what happiness can do :: When you decide to be 100% responsible for your own happiness, you empower yourself to create more happy experiences in your life. By doing this, you take the pressure off your partner to produce all your happiness for you. An additional benefit is that your happy vibration will be contagious, which will positively influence the energy of your love partner. When we choose to be responsible for our own happiness, we are less likely to be nit-picky over our partner's idiosyncrasies, and more focused on the parts of them that make us feel happy.

real world result :: Next time your partner forgets to call or comes home late for a dinner that you've been preparing all day; your happy mood will absorb the impact of what might otherwise seem like a careless act on his part. Because you're in a happy place, you can then allow yourself to sit in the observer's seat and hear your partner's explanation without criticizing and judging him. This ability to listen and understand him without judgment will allow his explanation to soothe any fear that may have surfaced so that you can continue to enjoy him and your day.

money ::

Our ability to manifest our worth financially is based totally on our belief system. If we believe that we are a victim of life or hold a poverty mentality, those thoughts that support that idea will surely make us feel unhappy. These unhappy feelings close down our connection to source energy and our creativity, slowing down the flow of money to us.

what happiness can do :: While I know you can produce money without being happy, choosing to be happy increases your imagination and creativity to come up with even grander ideas for making even more money. When you are happy, your ideas, choices and performance all increase, which are all vital assets that increase your ability to make money.

real world result :: When you are happy and you lose a client, rather than wallowing in all the potential stories you could make up about why they left, your high energy will motivate you to connect to the next opportunity. Being happy also enhances your job performance, because when you're riding high, angry bosses, flippant co-workers, and the delivery guy who can never seem to get to your office on time, don't bother you as much. This is because your happy energy allows you to sit more firmly in the observer's seat, and not take anything personally. This attitude helps you to navigate your career choices better, increasing your opportunities to be promoted right up the corporate ladder, according to your beliefs.

a look into my experience with happiness

By now, you may be thinking the same type of thoughts that crossed my mind when I first started learning about happiness, and how it really influences our lives. I used to think things like *"This all sounds a little "woo-woo" or too good to be true. How can my beliefs and choosing to be happy really change my life?"* Well, let me share with you a little bit of my experience. Outside of my spiritual training, building a personal belief for me began by increasing my awareness to include the idea that choosing to be in a "happy emotional frequency" would in fact, positively impact how I experienced life. Then as I applied the concept more intentionally to my life, I experienced positive results in those areas I desired. My own experience with this concept then further compelled me to develop several success techniques that would provide me with quantifiable results that were equal to my beliefs.

a look into my experience with happiness

Did I immediately feel like a "Rock Star" or have my life change overnight? No! However, when I allowed myself to be still and focus my energy on being happy, I would notice a subsequent increase in the quality of my thought stream, which always left me feeling better than when I didn't make the effort. Therefore, I chose to do it more often, and the more I practiced being happy, the easier it was to consciously get into that space. After doing this consciously for a while, it became a habitual way of thinking. Then, over the course of several years (yep, years), I noticed that the ideas and thoughts that once scared me no longer even entered my thought stream, which signaled to me that my mind had undergone a transformation, where I went from feeling vulnerable to the whims of life to someone who consciously created a beautiful reality.

manifesting happiness without emotional attachments

Every moment of every day you experience the manifestation of your beliefs, thoughts, and feelings in a physical world that reflects them back to you through your experienced reality. This is why I encourage you to do your best to maintain your baseline emotion of happiness as much as you are able, for it is by staying in this place that you can choose the best thoughts to think to create your desired experience. Reason being is this: when you choose to be happy first, you don't become as attached to the outcome of situations. If you are attached to an outcome to produce your happy feelings, it leaves you that much more susceptible to sadness or disappointment in the event that things don't go as you planned.

"But Morgan, you said that I'm an emotional being. So then, what do I do when I feel those other feelings? It sounds to me like you're talking about suppressing them to be happy."

In no way, shape, or form do I suggest that you suppress your feelings and try to fake happiness, as this is much like taking moldy bread and trying to make it a sweet treat by serving it with cake frosting. Yuck! If you suppress your negative feelings by repeating positive affirmations over and on top of them, you are giving focus to two or more different thought streams, which can only then produce a reality that is congruent with your blend of beliefs. Hence, this type of conflicting thought stream can only deliver chaotic experiences to you because your physical reality is being created according to the up and down quality of your thought stream and energy.

As I mentioned earlier, your feelings are an integral part of your internal compass, and they are not to be suppressed or ignored, as their purpose is to show you when your thoughts are going off track from what you desire. That said, just because you are signaled to feel a certain emotion - fear, sadness, anger, etc., it doesn't mean you have to give full focus and expression to it. Part of becoming Princess Charming means learning how to acknowledge your feelings as they relate to the experience you're having, so that you can redirect your thoughts if they are not aligned with your desired reality. Therefore, you can allow yourself to feel loss, guilt, rejection or anxiety as a signal that your thoughts are going off track without getting attached and falling into a debilitating depression over it, and still have a valid emotional experience. Practicing feeling your feelings from the perspective of the "happy observer" will help you to avoid emotional 'black holes' and the subsequent breakdown they create in your reality.

I do want to acknowledge that if you are someone who currently experiences yourself as being very emotional, the idea of implementing this concept of feeling your feelings from a happy or observer's perspective may feel very awkward. As someone who is empathetic, intuitive, and highly sensitive to the world around me, I understand how challenging it can be to learn to navigate what may seem like huge emotions initially. If this is you, I want to tell you that you can do this - you can get to a place where happiness is your consistent baseline emotion, especially when you really digest the fact that it's your thoughts that generate those feelings in the first place.

No matter where you fall on the emotional sensitivity scale, your emotions and how you choose to feel them has a direct effect on your ability to create your fairy tale as you wish. This is because, to the degree that you react or give energy to any emotion, and the thoughts that generated it, the deeper you will experience that feeling. Therefore, while indulging your emotions won't necessarily wreck your life, a pattern of giving focus to those thoughts that are counter to your desired reality will continue to create physical experiences that reflect and deepen your understanding of the feeling you're expressing internally. In other words, if you get sad while watching a movie and you let that sadness permeate your system for a certain amount of time, you will become more aware of things around you that make you feel sad in your world. This increased focus on sadness will continue to inspire ideas in your thought stream that guide you towards more experiences that reflect your beliefs of sadness back to you. The same is true when you experience something that brings you joy - your joyful mood will continue to feed you a thought stream full of creative ideas that will help you create experiences of joy in your physical reality. Because emotions are energy, that when given focus to, influence our reality, we must aspire to manifest feelings of happiness without emotional attachments towards how that happiness shows up.

what happens when your thoughts move faster than your beliefs?

I've noticed an interesting occurrence take place when people begin to understand how their thoughts create their feelings, which then inspires their choices and actions. As they begin to live more consciously, they become increasingly aware of the inspiration all around them, which supports their happy feelings. While you might assume successfully applying this principle would always produce feelings of euphoria, this is not always the case to the person newly experiencing it. Many times, when someone begins experiencing the effects of consciously creating their world, they can get so overwhelmed in their success that it actually triggers their ego to try and manage things. To the degree in which your ego gets involved, you will feel influenced to make choices that you believe will make you look or feel good in a future moment but, are usually hard to achieve because they're so far off from your current reality.

What we experience when our ego takes over is what I like to call an "inflated thought stream." This occurs because rather than staying in the moment, and focusing on being happy, we fall back into our old tendencies of only letting ourselves feel happy once the desired outcome has been achieved. Hence, the happy thought stream that was once creating our desired reality is now challenged. This challenge to our thought stream causes us to feel even more uncertain about our ability to create our desired reality, further encouraging our ego towards tactics of trying to force things to happen in order to soothe our fears.

This forceful energy then influences us to make choices that we believe will make us feel happy, but are rooted in the fear of lack and limitation, causing a breakdown in our reality. The two areas I see this happening in most with the majority of the women that I encounter are in their career or business, and in their pursuit of finding Prince Charming.

career and business :: One of the most common challenges that I see entrepreneurial and career women face is how they go about generating the thoughts and ideas that will create their happily ever after professionally. In the role of the entrepreneur, this often looks like trying to force a newly formed business to look as successful as its biggest competitors overnight, instead of enjoying each stage of the process, like nurturing a new baby. In the corporate professional, this seems to happen by micro-managing career choices that extend five and ten years into the future, which is the ego's way of trying to protect you from being hurt in a reality that doesn't yet exist. While both of these courses of action may give the person choosing them momentary peace about what they're going to create in their future, it can often leave them feeling limited and frustrated with their current reality. The reason this happens is because whenever we set an intention that is "bigger than where we are" or "far off in the future," we can't help but witness the disconnect between how our life is in the present, and the way we really want it to be. In witnessing this disconnect, we often develop various fears around the probability of it happening, and typically struggle with having enough patience to allow our desired reality to manifest.

prince charming :: This one happens time and again, and if it hasn't happened to you, I'm pretty sure it's happened to one of your family members or friends. You meet "him," the last man you will ever kiss and the father of your children, and it's only your second date. Nonetheless, and regardless of the fact that he's never mentioned wanting marriage or kids, you start creating your future together by talking up the relationship to your friends, checking out venues for weddings, and perusing baby naming books. Then, after dating awhile, you begin to discover all the things you didn't know about him, and when some of those things don't exactly match your happily ever after story line, you experience feelings of disappointment, and in some instances, anger.

If you choose to nurture these thoughts and feelings of frustration and disappointment, rather than seeing how it was your projections that are now causing you frustration, they can expand to such a state in your awareness as to create a breakdown in the relationship. Whether it's pressuring him about if and when you're getting married and or having children or nagging him about doing all the things you believe he should be doing if he loved you. Your increasing focus on only feeling happy with your partner once this future commitment has occurred, sabotages the relationship in the present by getting ahead of yourself in consciousness.

glass slipper insight :: If you can't see what thoughts to think next to create your reality as you desire, then you're projecting too far into the future and it's time to rewind your thought stream back to a point in time where you can see clearly. As it is by refocusing your thoughts back to the present, which gives you the ability to feel grateful and happy about all the things in your world that are aligned with your desires, increasing the experience of them in your reality.

Anything you currently desire first started off as an original idea in your thought stream, and in order for you to experience it in your physical reality, you must go through a certain evolutionary process of being. Just like a fruit tree that has to go through a process of seed to stem, and then tree to leaves before it can even begin to bear fruit, each step of your process to becoming Princess Charming is revealed to you through a prior experience in your reality. Therefore, if you try to force an outcome before you're ready, or you get ahead of yourself in your thinking, you will usually begin feeling as though your fairy tale is more like a nightmare than a dream. Hence, rather than getting ahead of yourself, and subsequently withholding your own good feelings from you until a later date, honor each present moment, as it holds the key to expanding your consciousness to the next stage in creating your desired reality.

This I promise you if you set an intention, and then focus on experiencing that intention, day after day, never deviating from your goal, you will experience your desire, or better, according to your belief. When you fully comprehend this, and I mean to the degree where you feel it and believe it deep within yourself, you will see how you can consciously create reality... and therefore, make it the way you want it to be.

is there more to life than happiness & bliss

Yes, there's gratitude! Choosing to be grateful is the key to feeling your happiness and bliss. When you choose to be in a state of gratitude or appreciation for who you are, you shift your perspective that much closer to that of Source Energy or the ultimate observer. I use the term ultimate observer as a reference to Source Energy as the Infinite Intelligence that is aware of all, holds a pure love vibration, and thus, is fearless. Therefore, when we allow ourselves to tune into the emotional frequency of gratitude, we are most like source energy, able to create our desired reality without fear influencing our thought stream.

When you choose to be grateful, your expanded state of awareness increases the quality of your thought stream to include ideas that inspire you to feel happy more easily. By focusing your intention on being grateful for your life, you direct your mind to create or find those experiences that you can feel grateful for. This process immediately, and over the course of time, can significantly increase the quality of your life. "How?" you ask; because we cannot feel gratitude and anything that resembles fear at the same moment in time. For example, pretend that you are a parent, looking at a painting done by your five-year-old.

While observing the art piece from a place of gratitude that your child is now at a stage where they could create it, your mind wouldn't be looking for things about it to criticize. Your mindset would be directed towards appreciating them and their work, which you would demonstrate with praise for their efforts and love for their expression of being.

Can you see how this shift towards appreciation for your life could change your entire paradigm for the better? Just think, if you could shift your perspective to one closer to that of the ultimate observer, or if it's easier to think of, a parent to your inner child, you would open the door to seeing each created experience in your life as a part of your process to becoming Princess Charming. This appreciation, when fully felt, would allow you to easily forgive and almost see as gifts, what you currently deem as past wrongs. I know you may be thinking that there are situations in your past that could never be thought of as a gift, and I understand why you may feel this way. Therefore, you may want to begin by thinking of these experiences as being life lessons, showing you where your thoughts were "off course," by reflecting your negative beliefs back to you, so that you could course correct. When you allow yourself to see things this way, you will discover that each encounter you've ever had was directing you in the ways that you needed to expand your consciousness in a particular direction, in order to experience yourself the way you were intended, which is love, peace, and happiness.

Before we close our time together, I want to take a moment to express my gratitude to you. I want to thank you for having the courage to go through this journey - and for allowing me to be a part of your happily ever after. This life that we experience is only a reflection of our beliefs, as the point of creating our happily ever after is so that we feel our beliefs have valid meaning. Therefore, as you go out into this world and begin more consciously creating your reality, I want to you to remember first and foremost, the greatest key to becoming Princess Charming is being happy.

glass slipper insight :: Now the pen is REALLY in your hand. How will you create your own happiness story? What will you choose to believe about who you are, as you manifest moment to moment the cherished memories that make up the fairy tale of your life?

I invite you now to write your fairy tale, as you want it to manifest before you, with your perfect health and wellness, a life-partner that fulfills your deepest fantasies, a career or professional endeavor that allows you to express your creative self at full capacity, and a home and life that exceeds what are currently your wildest dreams.

It is for you that I wrote this so that from this day forward, you would have one more way to create your happily ever after and a life of your own design as Princess Charming.

_____
_____
_____
_____
_____
_____
_____
_____
_____

You will only see it in your reality when it's congruent with your beliefs.

~ M

Footnotes

www.naturalnews.com

www.healthitude.net

www.responsibletechnology.org

www.everydayhealth.com

www.webmd.com

www.breastcancerfund.org

acknowledgements

When it comes to completing a book like this, none of us does it alone. Whether it's emotional support from family and friends, inspirational stories from our clients and colleagues, or FABULOUS Chai tea lattes from the barista at the local coffee house - each makes a valuable contribution to our ability to take a vision and make it a reality and for those of you who showed up in my world, I am grateful.

While I know there are far more people that contributed to this book than I can possibly list here, I would like to offer my very deep appreciation to the following few people who truly sacrificed to see the manifestation of this book:

ASHLEY MURPHY - Without your support, belief, reflection, edits, and support, I wouldn't have been able to push through the last but necessary "challenges" I had to finally finishing this book.

NICOLE MORSE - Just knowing I had your "legal" eyes watching over me – dotting every "I" and crossing every "T" - gave me the comfort I needed to know that I could create freely, and that someone would be there to catch anything that wasn't coming out how I wanted it to be.

LATONYA BLACK GILLIARD – Thank you for "seeing" me. My heart, my soul and all the things I would need, including your support, belief and expertise, to finally make this a book people could hold in their hands.

JAMIL THEODORE - You are the rock in my world. It is because of you that I have learned to balance growing roots, while keeping my wings to fly. Being your mother has made me love more, dig deeper, be more compassionate, and has finely tuned me in every way to make me a better person. You are a prince, and it is one of my greatest pleasures to be your mother. I love you! ~ 🖤 M

about the author

morgan b. mckean

If you're "stuck", angry, empty, depressed, or hurting... you're not alone. I can help.

I was born an Intuitive Empath, with a knack for helping people navigate the beautiful, yet sometimes murky waters of life, love, and intimate relationships. I first dipped my toe into spirituality and the human-potential movement at the age of six, and it has become a life-long love affair – which I now share with others, so they can heal their wounds and issues.

However, don't think because of my spiritual gifts and understandings that my life has been a bed of roses. Just like you, I've had self-esteem issues, have given into emotional eating, and have even been in a few abusive relationships.

And I've faced each of them successfully using the same insights, understandings, and techniques I now share in my private practice, on stage, and in the media. So, I can help others make the shift they need to get on with the business of healthy living.

Known for being a "Vitamin B12 Shot" for people's dreams, my intuitive teachings, and messages about love, success, and happiness have appeared in a variety of media outlets such as "TheDailyLove.com", "NPR Radio", "SheKnows Living", "Radio MD", "Ebony Magazine", "Coco Eco Magazine", and "MSN.com."

When Morgan isn't writing, speaking or doing intuitive readings, you will find her hanging out with her favorite person, her son, on Southern California's finest beaches. But you can connect with her on social media anytime. @morganbmckean on Instagram, Facebook and Pinterest, #becomingprincesscharming

www.ingramcontent.com/pod-product-compliance
Lightning Source LLC
Chambersburg PA
CBHW051044160426
43193CB00010B/1066